How to Manage

Books that make you better

Books that make you better – that make you *be* better, *do* better, *feel* better. Whether you want to upgrade your personal skills or change your job, whether you want to improve your managerial style, become a more powerful communicator, or be stimulated and inspired as you work.

Prentice Hall Business is leading the field with a new breed of skills, careers and development books. Books that are a cut above the mainstream – in topic, content and delivery – with an edge and verve that will make you better, with less effort.

Books that are as sharp and smart as you are.

Prentice Hall Business.
We work harder – so you don't have to.

For more details on products, and to contact us, visit
www.pearsoned.co.uk

JO OWEN

How to Manage

The art of making things happen

PEARSON

Prentice Hall

BUSINESS

Harlow, England • London • New York • Boston • San Francisco • Toronto • Sydney • Tokyo • Singapore • Hong Kong
Seoul • Taipei • New Delhi • Cape Town • Madrid • Mexico City • Amsterdam • Munich • Paris • Milan

PEARSON EDUCATION LIMITED

Edinburgh Gate
Harlow CM20 2JE
Tel: +44 (0)1279 623623
Fax: +44 (0)1279 431059
Website: www.pearsoned.co.uk

First published in Great Britain in 2006

ISBN: 978-0-273-70975-6

British Library Cataloguing-in-Publication Data
A catalogue record for this book is available from the British Library

Library of Congress Cataloging-in-Publication Data
Owen, Jo.
  How to manage / Jo Owen.
    p. cm.
  Includes index.
  ISBN-13: 978-0-273-70975-6 (alk. paper)
  ISBN-10: 0-273-70975-5 (alk. paper)
   1. Management--Handbooks, manuals, etc. 2. Leadership--Handbooks,
manuals, etc
  I. Title.

  HD31.15.o94 2006
  658--dc22

                                                          2006050105

10 9 8 7 6 5 4 3 2
10 09 08 07

Typeset in 9.5pt Iowan by 70
Printed and bound in Great Britain by Bell & Bain Ltd, Glasgow

The Publisher's policy is to use paper manufactured from sustainable forests.

Contents

1 Introduction and summary: real managers for the real world 1
   IQ: rational management 5
   EQ: emotional management 7
   PQ: political management 8
   MQ: the management quotient 9

2 IQ skills: dealing with problems, tasks and money 13
   2.1 Starting at the end: *focus on outcomes* 18
   2.2 Achieving results: *performance and perceptions* 22
   2.3 Making decisions: *acquiring intuition fast* 25
   2.4 Solving problems: *prisons and frameworks* 32
   2.5 Strategic thinking: *floors, romantics and the classics* 47
   Financial skills 54
   2.6 Setting budgets: *the politics of performance* 55
   2.7 Managing budgets: *the annual dance routine* 58
   2.8 Managing costs: *minimising pain* 60
   2.9 Surviving spreadsheets: *assumptions, not maths* 67
   2.10 Knowing numbers: *playing the numbers game* 69

3 EQ skills: dealing with people 75
   3.1 Motivating people: *creating willing followers* 79
   3.2 Influencing people: *how to sell anything* 84
   3.3 Coaching: *no more training* 96
   3.4 Delegating: *doing better by doing less* 99
   3.5 Handling conflict: *from FEAR to EAR* 102
   3.6 Giving informal feedback: *making the negative positive* 109
   3.7 Managing yourself: *personal EQ* 113
   3.8 Using time effectively: *activity versus achievement* 119
   3.9 Surviving the management marathon: *from days to decades* 130
   3.10 Learning the right behaviours: *what managers really want* 142

4 PQ skills: making things happen 153

4.1 The seven key power sources: *building a power base* 156

4.2 Acquiring power: *shining a light on the dark arts* 161

4.3 Building power networks: *becoming irreplaceable* 175

4.4 Using power: *setting your agenda* 181

4.5 The art of unreasonable management: *ruthlessness* 187

4.6 Saying 'no' to your boss: *surviving insanity* 193

4.7 Power and integrity: *from morality to survival* 195

4.8 Taking control: *telling stories* 196

4.9 Managing change: *people, not projects* 199

4.10 People and change: *through the valley of death* 206

5 MQ skills: managing your journey 221

5.1 Acquiring MQ: *how to learn success* 223

5.2 Employing MQ: *uses and abuses* 226

5.3 Decoding the success formula: *happy endings* 229

Index 233

Introduction and summary:

real managers for the real world

Management used to be much simpler: bosses bossed and workers worked. Managers used their brains and workers used their hands. Thinking and doing were separate activities. Those were good times for managers, but bad times for workers.

Somewhere it all started to go horribly wrong for managers. Workers slowly acquired more rights while managers lost their perks; workers got shorter working hours, managers had to work even longer hours. And while workers got the benefits of the 24/7 economy managers got the stress of being constantly shackled to the electronic fetters of email, texts and phone.

Management has become harder: not just harder, but also more ambiguous. Think for a moment about the rules of success and survival in your organisation. You can look in vain at the formal evaluation criteria to find the real rules of survival and success:

▶ How much risk should I take if I want to survive, and how much should I take if I want to succeed?

▶ What are the right projects and people to work with?

▶ When do I stand up and fight and when do I concede gracefully?

▶ How do things actually get done in this place?

▶ What are the bear traps to avoid?

There is no policy manual to tell you this, no training programme to help you. You are on your own when it comes to the important rules. Policy manuals only deal with the minor rules.

In practice, we discover the rules of survival and success by comparing people who succeed and survive to those who struggle. And then we work out why they succeed, survive or struggle. Take a look and see who succeeds in your organisation. Hopefully, people who have a track record of success are among the winners. But in flat organisations knowing who was really responsible for what can be a challenge.

Most evaluation systems look for two sorts of characteristics, which are called many different things.

Traditionally, managers (who had the brains) were meant to be smarter than the workers (who had the hands). A good IQ, or intelligence quotient, helped. Many assessment systems still assess IQ. Entry into many business schools is still based on IQ, in the form of the GMAT (a common test). In companies, IQ is often presented as having problem solving skills, analytical capability, business judgement and insight.

Being a brain on sticks is not enough to manage. Managing is about getting things done. Many smart people with high IQ are too clever to make anything happen. Most companies look for good interpersonal skills, or good EQ – emotional quotient. This will be dressed up as team work, adaptability, interpersonal effectiveness, charisma, ability to motivate and similar code words for EQ.

Now use the criteria of IQ and EQ to see who succeeds and fails. You should find quite a few managers with good IQ and EQ: smart (IQ) and nice (EQ) managers exist despite the media stereotypes. But you will also find plenty of smart and nice people who lead lives of quiet underachievement in the backwaters of the organisation: liked by all and going nowhere fast. Meanwhile there are plenty of successful managers who are not so smart and not so nice who rise to the top, using the smart and nice managers as doormats on their way to the executive suite.

Something is missing. It helps to have good IQ and EQ, but it is not enough. Another hurdle has come into place for managers to jump. As ever, things are getting tougher, not easier, for managers.

The new hurdle is about political savvy or PQ – political quotient. PQ is partly about knowing how to acquire power. Even more, it involves knowing how to use power to make things happen. This places it at the heart of management, which is about making things happen through other people.

Of course, all managers have always needed some degree of PQ. But in the command and control hierarchies of the past, it did not require much PQ to make things happen: an order was normally enough. In today's world of flat and matrix organisations, power is more diffused and ambiguous. Managers cannot do things without building alliances, getting help and support and reaching out beyond their formal areas of authority. Many of the resources they need will not even exist in their own organisation. Managers need PQ more than ever before to achieve their ends.

Successful managers are three dimensional: they have IQ, EQ and PQ. Each of these capabilities is a series of skills which can be learned. You do not have to be academically smart to be a good manager: many academic institutions are full of smart people and bad management. *How to Manage* shows how you can be managerially smart without having to be academically smart. Similarly, EQ and PQ represent skills which all managers can learn.

How to Manage lays out the managerial skills behind IQ, EQ and PQ. It shows how you can build your capabilities to survive and succeed in the revolution. It cuts through the noise of the daily management struggle and the babble of management theory to focus on the critical skills and interventions managers need. It shows what you have to do and how you have to do it in a world which is tougher and more complex than ever.

As a first step in understanding the revolution, we will look at how the revolution came about and where it is taking us.

IQ: rational management

As long as there has been civilisation, there has been management – even if no one realised it at the time. Management only started to evolve as a discipline in its own right with the Industrial Revolution: large-scale operations required large-scale organisation. Early management organisation and strategy was based on military strategy and organisation: classic command and control.

Slowly, industrial management evolved away from military management. Just as Newton discovered the laws of physics, so managers went in search of the elusive formula for business and management success. It is a formula which academics still search for, although successful entrepreneurs do not need a theory to succeed. Scientific management was an early attempt to bottle success.

The high priest of scientific management was Frederick Taylor who wrote *The Principles of Scientific Management* in 1911. Below is a flavour of his approach:

One of the very first requirements for a man who is fit to handle pig iron as a regular occupation is that he shall be so stupid and so phlegmatic that he more nearly resembles in his mental make-up the ox than any other type. The man who is mentally alert and intelligent is for this very reason entirely unsuited to what would, for him, be the grinding monotony of work of this character.

Taylor took a dim view of workers as a whole, believing that they would work as little as they could without getting punished. But his work was not based on pure opinion: it was also supported by close observation. This led to some ideas which were revolutionary at the time:

▶ Workers were allowed to rest because it made them more productive.

▶ Different types of person should be given different types of job because they would be more productive in the right jobs.

▶ Production lines, which break complicated jobs such as assembling cars or fast-food, maximise productivity and minimise the skills and costs of the employees required.

These lessons are still applied today.

The world of scientific, or rational, management was brought to life by Henry Ford's introduction of the moving production line for making cars. Between 1908 and 1913 he perfected the concept and started to produce the Model-T, which he called with great marketing aplomb 'a motor car for the great multitude'. Some 15 million Model-Ts had rolled off his assembly lines by 1927, bringing cars to the masses and sweeping away the cottage industry of craftsmen custom building cars at great expense.

Rational management is alive and kicking even in the 21st century: it still exists on car assembly lines, in fast-food restaurants and in call centres where hapless operatives work to scripts which make them little more than machines. Many companies have taken the next logical step and removed the humans completely so that customers are left dealing with automated systems.

EQ: emotional management

The world of rational, scientific management was relatively simple: it was based on observation and cold calculation.

Then it all started becoming complicated for managers.

Somewhere along the line, someone discovered that workers were not mere units of production, and possibly even of consumption. They had hopes, fears, feelings and even the occasional thought. They were, in fact, human beings. This really confused matters for managers. They not only had to handle problems, they also had to handle people.

Over time, people became harder to handle. Workers became better educated and better skilled: they could now contribute more, but they also expected more. They became wealthier and more independent. The days of the one factory town were numbered: there were alternative forms of employment and a better welfare state for those who could not or would not find employment. Employers lost their coercive power. They could no longer demand loyalty; they had to earn it. Slowly, the workplace was moving from a culture of compliance to a culture of commitment.

The challenge for management was how to produce the high commitment workplace, engaging people's hopes instead of simply playing on their fears. Eighty-four years after Frederick Taylor published his book, Daniel Goleman appeared as the high priest of the new world of emotional management with *Emotional Intelligence: Why it can matter more than IQ* (1995). He was, in effect, popularising thinking which had been emerging for decades. As early as 1920, E.L. Thorndike of Columbia University had been writing about 'social intelligence'. For a long time, thinkers had realised that smart thinking (high IQ) was not directly correlated with life success: other things seem to be important.

In the workplace, experiments with emotional intelligence (EQ, not IQ) had long been taking place. The Japanese in particular made great strides in involving workers properly, even on car production lines, through new movements such as *kaizen* (continuous improvement). Perhaps ironically, they took much of their inspiration from an American, W. Edwards

Deming. Deming's ideas only gained acceptance in America when the Japanese started to decimate the US auto industry with the help of his ideas.

By the end of the 20th century, the manager's job had become far more complicated than it had been at the end of the 19th century. Twentieth century managers needed to be just as smart as their predecessors of a hundred years before. They needed EQ (emotional quotient) to deal with people as much as they needed IQ to deal with problems. Most managers found that they could be good at one or the other: few managers have genuinely good IQ *and* EQ. The performance bar for effective management had been raised dramatically.

PQ: political management

Two-dimensional managers cannot exist, except as cartoon characters. Real people and real managers exist in three dimensions. The concepts of high IQ and EQ are good, but they are not sufficient to explain the success or otherwise of different sorts of managers. Something is missing.

The first clue to finding the missing piece of the puzzle is to recognise that organisations are set up for conflict. This is a surprise to some academics who think that organisations are set up for collaboration. In reality, managers have to fight for a limited pot of their organisation's time, money and budget. There are always more needs than there are resources. Internal conflict is the way that these priorities are decided with marketing, production, service, HR and the different products and regions all slugging it out to get their fair share of the cake.

For many managers, the real competition is not in the marketplace. The real competition is sitting at a desk nearby fighting for the same promotion and the same bonus pool.

The second clue to the missing piece of the puzzle is to look at who wins and loses in these corporate contests for budget, time, pay and promotion. If we are to believe the high IQ and EQ theory then all the smart and nice people should get to the top. Casual observation of most organisations shows that this is not true. Smart and nice people do not always win: many disappear off the corporate radar screen entirely or live as quiet under-achievers. On the other side of the coin, most of us have experienced senior managers who are neither bright nor pleasant, and yet they mysteriously rise into positions of power and prominence.

Clearly, there is something more than IQ and EQ.

A short chat around the water cooler is often enough to discover what is missing. Round the water cooler, conversation often turns to who is going up or down the corporate escalator, who is in and out, who is doing what to whom, what the big emerging opportunities are, and what the emerging death star projects are and how to avoid them. Such conversations show that humans are not only social animals: we are also political animals.

Politics is unavoidable in any organisation. Nor is politics new. Shake-speare's *Julius Caesar* is politics dramatised. Machiavelli's *The Prince* is the Renaissance guide to successful political management. Politics has always been there, but it has been seen as a slightly dirty topic, not fit for academic analysis or for corporate training programmes. Caesar's murder shows what happens when you do not pay proper attention to the politics of the organisation.

IQ and EQ are not sufficient to deal with such politics. There is a constant contest for control and for power. The endless need for change is not just about changing individuals: it is about changing the power balance in the organisation. These are deeply political acts for which the successful man-ager needs deep political and organisational skills.

MQ: the management quotient

Perhaps it is now time to recognise that real managers are three dimen-sional. In addition to high IQ and EQ, they need high PQ: political quotient. If there is such a thing as a success formula in management, it might be summarised as:

$$MQ = IQ + EQ + PQ$$

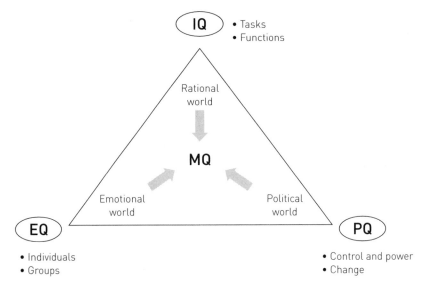

Components of MQ

MQ is your management quotient. To increase your MQ, you need to build up IQ, EQ and PQ. The success formula is easy to state, hard to achieve.

MQ is about management practice, not management theory. *How To Manage* shows how you can use MQ as a simple framework to:

▶ assess your own management potential

▶ assess team members and help them identify how they can improve

▶ identify and build the core skills you need to succeed

▶ identify the rules of survival and success in your organisation.

There are countless ways to apply the MQ formula and to succeed or to fail. Each person develops and applies IQ, EQ and PQ in different ways to suit different situations. Each person's management style is as unique as their DNA. *How To Manage* does not provide a formula for producing managerial clones. You deserve better than that. It provides a set of frameworks and tools to help you understand and deal with typical management challenges.

Some people treat frameworks as prisons: they mindlessly apply the same formula to every situation. Others use frameworks as scaffolding around which they can build their own unique management style. They adapt the tools to their unique circumstances. *How To Manage* helps you adapt the tools and frameworks by showing not just the theory, but also the reality of what works and, more importantly, what does not work. We all learn from experience, both positive and negative. This book crams thousands of years of cumulative experience from practising managers into a few pages. Use *How to Manage* well and you will be able to build your MQ to succeed on your own terms.

IQ skills:

dealing with problems, tasks and money

Being a smart manager is different from being a smart intellectual. Brilliant professors rarely emerge as great managers. Conversely, many of the best entrepreneurs today are people who did not trouble themselves with the time, expense and conformist thinking of an MBA: Bill Gates, Warren Buffet, Richard Branson and Steve Jobs are all MBA free zones.

Asking great managers what makes them great is an exercise in toadying and ingratiation which yields little more than platitudes and self-congratulation. I have tried it: it is not an exercise worth doing once, letting alone repeating. For the most part they will talk about things like 'experience' and 'intuition'. This is deeply unhelpful. You cannot teach intuition. Experience is a recipe for keeping junior managers junior until they have grown enough grey hairs to become part of the management club. I had to find out another way of discovering how managers thought, short of wiring them up to machines all day. So I did the next best thing: I decided to watch them work. Watching people work is invariably more congenial than actually doing the work.

Each person and each day is unique. Some people prefer face-to-face work rather than dealing through email; some days are totally consumed by a couple of big meetings, some people work longer and a few work less. But once we stripped away all these variances, we found these familiar patterns to a manager's working day:

▶ high fragmentation of time
▶ management of multiple agendas
▶ management of multiple constituencies and competing agendas
▶ constant flow of new information requiring reaction, change, adjustment
▶ low amounts of time working alone.

This is a pattern which is familiar to most managers. It has been compared to juggling while trying to run a marathon in a series of 100-metre sprints without dropping any of the balls. It is a world in which it is very easy to be busy but very difficult to make an impact. Activity is not a substitute for achievement. The challenge for managers today is to do less and achieve more.

At this point, pause to consider what you do not see in the normal management day:

▶ decision making using formal tools, such as Bayesian analysis and decision trees

▶ problem solving either by sitting alone and thinking deeply or by working in a group with a formal problem-solving technique

▶ formal strategic analysis of the business

Many MBA tools are notable by their absence from the daily lives of most managers: organisational and strategic theory go missing; financial and accounting tools remain functionally isolated within finance and accounting; marketing remains a mystery to most people in operations or IT.

The absence of these tools from most managers' days does not make them irrelevant. They may be used sparingly, but at critical moments. Most organisations would not survive long if all their managers were conducting non-stop strategic reviews of the business. But a good strategic review once in five years by the CEO can transform the business.

By now the search for the management mindset was becoming lost in the whirl of activity that is the standard management day. It looked like great managers did not need to be intellectually smart and did not need the standard intellectual and analytical tools that appear in books and courses. But it would be a brave person who accused Bill Gates and Richard Branson of being dumb. All the leaders and managers we interviewed were smart enough to get into positions of power and influence. They were smart, but not in the conventional way of schools. Management intelligence is different from academic intelligence.

We decided to dig deeper, thereby breaking the golden rule 'when in a hole, stop digging'. We hoped we were not digging a hole. We hoped we were digging the foundations of understanding the management mindset. We eventually found these foundations – explored in the following sections – all of which can be learned and acquired by any manager:

2.1   Starting at the end: focus on outcomes

2.2   Achieving results: performance and perceptions

2.3   Making decisions: acquiring intuition fast

2.4   Solving problems: prisons and frameworks – and tools

2.5   Strategic thinking: floors, romantics and the classics

2.6   Setting budgets: the politics of performance

2.7   Managing budgets: the annual dance routine

2.8   Managing costs: minimising pain

2.9   Surviving spreadsheets: assumptions, not maths

2.10 Knowing numbers: playing the numbers game

If we were being intellectually rigorous, not all of these skills might exist in a chapter on management IQ. But there is some method behind the randomness.

Outcome focus and achieving results (foundations 2.1 and 2.2) are included in this chapter because they are at the heart of the effective manager's mindset. The way an effective manager thinks is driven by the need to drive results and achieve outcomes. This creates a style of thinking which is highly pragmatic, fast-paced and quite unlike anything you normally find in textbooks and academia. It is about achievement, not activity.

Foundations 2.3 to 2.5 are classic IQ skills. There is a huge difference between how textbooks say managers should think and how they really think. Textbooks look for the perfect answer. Managers look for the practical answer. Practical is preferable to perfect. For many managers, the real problem is not even finding the answer: the real challenge is finding out the question. The really good managers spend more time working out what the question is, before attempting to find the pragmatic answer.

Foundations 2.6 to 2.10 could be called FQ – financial quotient. We expected to find that Finance and Accounting is 100 per cent IQ. We were 100 per cent wrong. In theory, financial management is a highly objective and intellectual exercise in which answers are either right or wrong: the numbers do or do not add up. For managers, the intellectual challenge is the minor part of the challenge. The major part of the challenge is not intellectual: it is political. Most financial discussions and negotiations are political discussions about money, power, resources, commitments and expectations. In many ways, financial management could better belong in the PQ (political quotient) chapter. Out of deference to financial theory, it is included in the IQ chapter.

In the sections which follow, we will pay our dues to theory. Theory is not useless: good theory creates a framework for structuring and understanding unstructured and complex issues. The main focus, however, is on the practice of how managers develop and deploy these IQ skills in practice.

2.1 Starting at the end: focus on outcomes

Managers have long been told 'first things first'. This is tautological nonsense: it depends on what you define as 'first'. In practice, managers do not start at the start. Effective managers start at the end.

For speed readers, let's repeat the message: *effective managers start at the end*.

Working backwards from the desired outcome, rather than shambling forwards from today is at the heart of how good managers think and work. This outcome focus is essential because it:

- ▶ gives clarity to and focuses on what is important
- ▶ pushes people to action, not analysis
- ▶ finds positive ways forward, rather than worrying about the past
- ▶ simplifies priorities
- ▶ helps to identify potential obstacles and avoid them.

Outcome focus is a relatively easy discipline to learn. It requires asking the same four questions time and time again:

1   What outcome do I want to achieve from this situation?

2   What outcome does the other person expect from this situation?

3   What are the minimum number of steps required to get there?

4   What are the consequences of this course of action?

Keep asking these four questions relentlessly and you will find the fog of confusion lifts from most situations, and you can drive a team to action.

1 What outcome do I want to achieve from this situation?

Asking this question drives us into action and gives people a sense of clarity and purpose. It is also a way of taking control of a situation and gaining benefit from it. It is a way of avoiding becoming dependent on other people's agendas, being purely reactive, or of slipping into analysis paralysis. Two examples will make the point:

Example one

A project was going horribly wrong: it threatened to go over time and budget. The team was having an inquest, which was rapidly turning into the normal blame game of 'he said, she said, I said no, she said. . .' Things were turning nasty. Then the team leader stopped the debate and asked: 'OK, we have two weeks left on the project. The question is this: what can we do in the next two weeks to achieve a satisfactory outcome?' Suddenly the debate turned from defensive analysis into a positive discussion about what the team could do. The leader had focused the team on outcomes and action, not on problems and analysis

Example two

The analyst had done a great job. She had compiled a mountain of data. The result was that her draft presentation was indigestible. Every piece of datum was so good it was hard to see what to leave out. So her manager asked her to focus on what she wanted to achieve from the presentation. The desired outcome was very simple: agree to a new project. Suddenly, it was easy to focus on a short story line which could persuade the decision maker about the project. The discussion was no longer 'what shall we leave out of the presentation?' but 'what is the minimum we need to include to make our case?'. About 90 per cent of the presentation disappeared into an appendix which was never read. She had learned that presentations and reports are not complete when there is nothing left to say or write: they are complete only when it is impossible to say or write any less. Brevity is much harder than length. Presentations and reports are like diamonds: they benefit greatly from good cutting.

2 What outcome does the other person expect from this situation?

Most managers are serving clients of some sort. Their client may be their boss, a colleague or an external partner. One way or the other, managers are supporting other people's agendas. Understanding what the other person wants is a very simple way of clarifying what the desired outcome of any situation is. Achieving clarity on this question enables the manager to:

▶ simplify and focus on the task in hand – the extraneous work quickly disappears

▶ predict and pre-empt problems and questions

▶ deliver appropriate outcomes to the other person.

Look back at the two examples above. In each case, the individuals concerned were able to understand what they needed to do by understanding what 'the other person' wanted:

▶ the project team became focused on the outcome for the client

▶ the analyst's presentation was focused on building a simple message for the person who needed to see the presentation.

3 What are the minimum number of steps required to get there?

There are plenty of people who make things complicated. While some people cannot see the wood for the trees, others cannot even see the trees for all the branches, twigs and leaves. Effective managers have a knack of making things simple. Given the increasing time pressure on all managers, this is an essential skill to have. Discovering the minimum number of steps requires asking a few more questions:

▶ What is the desired outcome (again)?

▶ Are there any short cuts: can I buy in a solution, get someone else to provide all or part of the solution, is there an authoriser who can short cut the normal approval channels?

▶ Does the 80/20 rule apply here: can I achieve 80 per cent of the result with just 20 per cent of the effort by focusing on the few customers who count, or the critical analysis that will really decide the issue, or by attacking the two big cost sinks that are causing the most problems?

▶ What are the critical dependencies? There is normally a logical order to events: billing comes after shipping comes after manufacturing comes after selling. Establishing this logical order breaks even the most daunting problem down into bite-sized chunks which people can manage.

4 What are the consequences of this course of action?

This question is about predicting risks, problems, unintended consequences and uncomfortable questions. If you can predict problems, you can pre-empt them. This is also the stage at which the manager may allow a little complexity to creep back into the course of action.

In theory, the shortest distance between two points is a straight line, except in non-Euclidean geometry: three-dimensional geometry is more complicated than three-dimensional management. In practice, management find that the fastest route is often not a straight line. When you are sailing against the wind, the fastest route between two points is a zigzag. Sailing straight into the wind gets nowhere. This is an experience most managers understand after they have tried to sail against the political winds in their organisation.

The easiest way to work out the consequences of most management actions is to understand who the major stakeholders are and how they will react: each stakeholder has a different perspective and will have different criteria and needs. The finance department will worry about affordability and payback; marketing will look at competitive reactions; sales will worry about price and positioning; HR will look at the staffing implications. Once you have a map of who is interested in what, you can then plot a zigzag through all the constituencies to make sure each one is able to satisfy their required needs.

2.2 Achieving results: performance and perceptions

Managers have to achieve results. Results are not always about delivering a profit: not everyone has P&L responsibility. Managers may be responsible for project outcomes, quality outcomes, costs, product design, development and delivery, and recruiting and training staff. There are endless possible results that managers may be responsible for. Ultimately, the test for a manager is to make sure you deliver those results. For better or for worse, many organisations do not look too closely at how results are achieved, unless there is immoral or illegal activity involved. Conversely, if a manager fails to deliver results, the manager fails. Results are better than excuses.

There are essentially five ways in which managers can achieve acceptable results:

1 Work harder

2 Work smarter

3 Fix the base line

4 Play the numbers game

5 Manage for results.

1 Work harder

This is an unpalatable truth in the era of work–life balance, which is shorthand for a wish to work less. This is also the 24/7 era when we are permanently attached to our various electronic tags which constrain us as much as a prisoner's leg irons: there is no escape. Working harder, however, is not a lasting solution. Given the ambiguous nature of most managerial work, bosses do not know how much effort each manager is really putting in. If you achieve results, the assumption is that you can do more. So the reward of working harder is to get more work. You only get less work when you can no longer deliver or you complain loudly enough.

2 Work smarter

This is the desired outcome of results obsession: we find ways of doing things betterfastercheaper. Betterfastercheaper is the essence of capitalism. When a manager achieves betterfastercheaper the ideal result is promotion. The more immediate consequence is normally the same as working harder: an increased workload rather than decreased working time.

3 Fix the baseline

Beating a soft target is easier than beating a tough target. Many managers realise that it is better to negotiate hard for one month securing a soft target than it is to work hard for 11 months trying to beat a tough target. Even CEOs do this: watch the frequency with which a new CEO discovers a black hole in the organisation's finances which require write offs and adjustments to the corporate goals. (See section 2.10 for details on fixing baselines.)

4 Play the numbers game

There is an annual ritual in most organisations called 'meet year-end budget'. Experienced managers know that this is coming, and they know that even if they are doing well, they are likely to be asked to deliver a little more in the last two months to make up for shortfalls elsewhere. This is where managers get creative. If they are doing well, they will hide spare budget for the inevitable year-end rainy day. If they are behind, they will use a combination of real actions on costs and whatever accounting smoke screens and mirrors can come to their support (see section 2.10 for more detail). This may appear cynical, but it is part of the reality of management survival.

Unintended consequences of results obsession

Results focus has some unintended consequences. In the public sector, targets obsession leads to awkward outcomes, for instance:

▶ Schools are ranked on students' test results: schools put pupils into the easiest subjects to pass to increase pass rates. They try to pre-

---

select students on ability so their overall results look good. Results improve, education does not.

▶ Hospitals are asked to reduce waiting times for operations: they use creative methods to move people off waiting lists and onto other sorts of list: and they require re-registration at frequent intervals so that people disappear off the list when they fail to re-register.

▶ Government needs to spend but also meet its debt targets, so it moves both spending and borrowing off its records by letting the private sector undertake major infrastructure projects (relating to hospitals, railways, etc). If the private sector tried the same techniques, the regulators would probably start calling.

The private sector is not much better. For instance:

▶ Banks reward loan officers on the volume of loans they make. Lending money to people is easy: getting it back is harder. By the time the bad debts mount up, the loan officers have received their bonus and moved on.

▶ Train companies and airlines extend the published flying time on routes (London to Paris is 20 minutes slower than 25 years ago) which then allows them to claim more of their flights arrive on time.

▶ London Underground has reduced service frequency on the Circle Line to 'improve customer satisfaction': this means that it can meet its published, but reduced, targets for the service being available. Ultimately, if it runs just one train an hour, it can achieve near 100 per cent service compliance and 100 per cent customer dissatisfaction.

The first four approaches all depend on the manager doing things. The role of the manager is to make things happen through other people. This leads to the fifth, managerial option.

5 Manage for results

Managers make things happen through other people. There is a huge difference between doing (working harder and smarter) versus managing (enabling other people to work harder and smarter). Managers who try to do it all themselves are not really managing and, in the long run, are condemned to fail. Management is a team sport. Managers need to have the right people tackling the right challenges the right way: the focus of this book is on how managers can make things happen through other people.

2.3 Making decisions: acquiring intuition fast

Decision making: principles

Good managers are often referred to as being decisive. 'Being decisive' is one of those vague management terms like 'professional', 'effective' or 'charismatic' that is very difficult to pin down, no one can teach and it is assumed that you either have it or you do not. We found that decisive managers typically show four specific behaviours:

1 *Bias for action over analysis*. Actions achieve results, analysis does not. Less analysis can often lead to a better solution because it forces discussion to focus on the big issues that make a big difference. Often, detail derails decision making.

2 *Prefer practical to perfect solutions*. Accept that the perfect solution does not exist. Find a solution which will work in practice, even if it is not perfect in theory. The perfect solution is the enemy of the good solution because the search for perfection leads to inaction. A good solution is fit for purpose and leads to action.

3 *Solve the problem with other people*. Use the collective knowledge, wisdom and experience of the organisation to gain insight. Use them to identify and avoid the major risks and pitfalls. But do not convert a problem-solving process into a political negotiation in which the solution is a fix designed to pacify everyone. The result will be the least offensive rather than the most effective solution.

4 *Take responsibility*. Where there are shared and unclear responsibilities, most organisations breathe a huge sigh of relief when one person steps

up and takes responsibility. 'The man (or woman) with the plan' becomes the person to follow. It is a defining moment which separates out leaders from followers: most people are very happy to follow.

These behaviours are hallmarks of a decisive manager, at least on minor matters such as sorting out late deliveries, staffing problems, budget arguments. But these useful instincts often desert managers when they are faced with a major decision. As the scale of the problem escalates, the number of people involved in it grows and the rational and political risks increase. Suddenly, managers become very risk averse. The manager's nightmare is to be held accountable for a decision which went wrong. To avoid this fate, managers seek refuge behind formal processes, exhaustive analysis and widespread consultation to optimise the decision and, more importantly, diffuse responsibility. Even if the decision turns out to be wrong, everyone was so involved in the process that they will find it difficult to pin the blame on one person. What should be a rational process (make a decision) becomes a political process (avoid blame for a potentially damaging solution).

The larger the decision, the more risk averse managers become.

A risky exercise

You are offered the chance to win $1,000 on a toss of a coin (a 50/50 chance, in theory). How much would you pay to play this game?

Most people will offer much less than $500, which should be the mean average payout from the game, if it is played enough times. Fear of loss outweighs the prospect of gain. Of course, make the game for 10 cents, and most people will happily play for five cents: risk aversion increases with the scale of the possible loss.

Managers are even more risk averse than the public. In general, the payoff from making a risky and correct decision is quite low. Your success may be derailed by other factors or claimed by other people, and it will probably have a minimal impact on your overall pay and promotion prospects. But the consequences of making a risky but incorrect decision are huge:

colleagues will make sure that the blame is pinned on you, and your reputation will suffer.

Decision-making traps

Analysis over action

Analysis is safe, action is risky. But analysis often throws up more challenges and more problems which require more analysis. Slowly the problem-solving exercise takes on a life of its own. No one can see through the thicket of challenges and problems which the analysis is throwing up. Paralysis through analysis becomes an unwelcome reality.

Seeking perfection over practicality

Faced with small problems, short cuts seem acceptable. But bigger problems deserve better solutions, and the biggest problems deserve perfect solutions. The perfect solution must also be the least risky solution. Except that in the messy world of management, there is no perfect solution. Any solution tends to be a trade-off between two unacceptable alternatives. No good solution exists on paper: good solutions only exist in reality.

Hiding behind other people

It is far better to be wrong collectively than it is to be wrong individually: no one wants to run the risk of being asked to don the corporate equivalent of the dunce's cap. In some organisations it is better to be wrong collectively than right individually: being right against the grain is seen to be disruptive to the team. The search for collective responsibility is natural risk avoidance. Collective responsibility requires consensus, which rarely represents the best solution. The consensus solution represents the least unacceptable solution to each constituency: it is a political fix. The purpose of involving other people is not to achieve a consensus, it is to gain insight. Ultimately, one person needs to own both the problem and the solution. They should use other people to gain insight and drive to action, but not to hide behind them in case things go wrong later.

Shedding responsibility

Responsibility for large problems, and their solutions, is often shared among several departments. This can lead to an unseemly game of 'pass the blame': no one really wants to be associated with causing the problem. Analysis of the problem becomes bogged down in an autopsy around what went wrong, rather than what the solution should be.

Decision making in practice

There are many decision-making and problem-solving tools available to managers and: these are covered in the next chapter. In practice, managers rarely use such formal tools. Instead, there are three questions managers ask themselves which normally yield a practical answer:

1   Is there a pattern I recognise here?

2   Who does this decision matter to, and why?

3   Does someone know the answer anyway?

1 Is there a pattern I recognise here?

Pattern recognition is what managers often refer to as intuition or experience. Unlike intuition, pattern recognition can be learned. Pattern recognition is simply a matter of observing what works and what does not work in different situations. If you recognise a familiar pattern, you will be able to predict what actions will work or fail. You will appear to have intuitive business sense.

Learning to recognise patterns

Advertising is a curious world where the creativity of advertisers has to meet the disciplines of the marketplace. Good advertising can transform a brand; poor advertising can kill it. Either way, it costs a fortune to make and to air. The challenge for clients, who pay the advertising agencies, is to know whether their spending is going to work.

Proctor & Gamble (P&G), one of the world's largest advertisers, does not rely on intuition. It has built up huge experience and has learned patterns of success and failure. Young brand managers have to acquire this intuition, or pattern recognition, fast. Inside the major offices of P&G there is a dark

---

room where the secrets of advertising intuition are learned. On appointment, the first thing a brand manager will do is to go into this room and acquire the knowledge. He or she will do this by reviewing tapes of all the advertising the brand has aired in perhaps the past 50 years. Watching 50 years of Daz advertising is like watching a social history of Britain. And for each piece of advertising, there are key statistics to show how well it fared.

After a few hours of watching such advertising, even the rawest marketing manager acquires an uncanny ability to look at 30 seconds of advertising and to predict how well it scored and performed. This is intuition acquisition on speed. It cuts through theory and shows what works in practice.

Pattern recognition comes into play when the manager realises that he or she is going to be responsible for making a decision. If it is a familiar pattern, it is normally an easy decision (see the box above for a typical example).

Effective managers observe and learn from everyday situations to build up their own knowledge of what does and does not work in their own organisation. We may not have the luxury of reviewing 50 years of people managing conflicts, negotiating, influencing people or problem solving, but good observation builds our skills, helps our pattern recognition and helps us appear to have excellent business sense and intuition.

Pattern recognition can be acquired and learned in a range of decision-making conditions:

▶ Competitive reactions: long-established competitors know how each other will react, without the need for collusion which would break anti-trust laws. In many markets there is a price leader from whom all competitors take their cues. If the leader raises prices, everyone else follows. If there is a temporary price reduction for a promotion, competitors ignore it. If the price reduction is permanent, competitors follow. This makes pricing decisions across companies very simple: it is called 'follow my leader'.

▶ Buying decisions: Philip Green is a billionaire retail entrepreneur who owns several fashion chains in the UK. When he looks at a rack of clothing he is reputed to be able to cost each item accurately and to establish its proper retail price at a glance. The buyer who is perceived to have overpaid for any line items is likely to have an uncomfortable discussion with the boss. Green is able to do this because he has seen thousands of racks of clothing over several decades of retail experience. His expert judgement is based on piling up the experience. He can demonstrate intuitively good sense on buying matters because he has seen the purchasing patterns so many times before.

▶ Managing people, including bosses, is largely about pattern recognition. We quickly have to learn what turns people on and off in terms of working style, risk appetite, people versus task focus, process versus outcome focus and more. No pattern is the right pattern: from the manager's perspective the point is to learn what works with different people.

If a decision fits into a familiar pattern, then most managers have the confidence to make a decision. The P&G brand manager will approve the development of a new campaign based on judgement, without recourse to expensive and time-consuming market research. Green can buy effectively because he recognises the patterns unique to his trade.

2 Who does this decision matter to, and why?

Decision making is as much about politics as it is about reason. Managers need solutions which lead to action: the perfect solution which is not acted upon is useless. Decisions only lead to action if people support the decision. This means that managers will ask 'who?' as much as 'what?'

There are essentially four possibilities here, each with a different outcome in terms of decision making:

1   *The decision is most important to a team member*. If possible, back the team member. Coach them and encourage them to arrive at a decision. Do not let them become dependent on you for making all their decisions: they will not grow professionally and you will die under an avalanche of requests for decisions.

2   *The decision is important for one of your bosses*. If you understand his or her agenda, it should be clear what the preferred decision is: frame the problem and the solution, and sell it to the boss. If the choice is unclear, work through the issue with the boss.

3   *The decision is important to another colleague.* Long term, managers need alliances and supporters across an organisation, so talk to the colleague and find a mutually advantageous solution. Help them: win a friend.

4   *The decision is important to you and your agenda.* If the choice is obvious, decide. If it is not, get help (see below).

This is decision making which is free of any problem-solving skills. The key skills are around understanding the agendas of bosses, colleagues and your team, and framing the decision to support those agendas. For this reason, many decisions emerge gradually over time. A consensus slowly builds, small actions are taken which favour one choice over another and gradually a preferred course of action emerges. This fits with the apparently chaotic schedule of many managers: lots of small interactions over the day help them understand others' agendas, sell an agenda, gather information and migrate slowly towards a series of decisions.

3 Does someone know the answer anyway?

Management is a team sport. No single manager is expected to know all the answers, but they may be expected to find all the answers.

For more complex decisions, no one knows the answer. But many different individuals in finance, marketing, operations, IT, sales and HR will hold part of the answer. They each hold one piece of the jigsaw and the job of the manager is to put the pieces together. This is both an intellectual process (discovering the best answer) and a political process (building a coalition in support of the emerging answer). This can take time. It may require several iterations before consensus can emerge and all the different agendas can be aligned.

In Japan, this consensus-based decision making is called *nemawashi*. The idea is to build agreement to the decision before the decision-making meeting. Carry out the initial conversations in private. This is critical. As soon as anyone has taken a position in public, they will feel the need to defend it at all costs, rather than lose face by changing their position. In private, you can have much more open and flexible conversations: real issues can be discussed, agendas can be aligned and commitment can be built. The more you talk the more you will understand the politics of the decision and the views of different stakeholders. You will gain more insight into the nature of the decision: you will better understand what the real challenge is, what the different options are and the consequences of each option. The more you talk, the more likely it is that a consensus will emerge around one preferred solution.

The final decision-making meeting still has relevance, but it is not about making a decision. It is about confirming in public to all the stakeholders that there really is consensus and agreement. It builds confidence and legitimises the decision which has already been made in private.

2.4 Solving problems: prisons and frameworks

Problem solving is sometimes thought to be the preserve of people who are brains on sticks. In reality, brains on sticks are precisely the wrong sort of people for solving most management problems: really smart people search fruitlessly for the non-existent perfect solution so they achieve nothing. A workable solution is preferable to the perfect solution because it leads to action.

Three principles lie behind effective problem solving:

1   Know your problem.

2   Focus on causes, not symptoms.

3   Prioritise the problems.

1 Know your problem

All students are given strict briefing before sitting any exam: 'Make sure you answer the question.' This is remarkably obvious advice, which is remarkably often ignored – with catastrophic consequences. The same advice needs to be given to all managers: 'Make sure you answer the question.' At least with school exams, the question is clear. In business, no one hands out an exam paper: you are expected to know what the exam question is without being told.

At junior levels of management, the exam questions are often pretty clear. They tend to be expressed as simple performance goals: sell more product, trade more profitably, bill more personal time. As managers continue their careers, clarity reduces and ambiguity increases. The goal may be clear (make your profit target) but the means to the end are not clear. It pays to fight the right battles the right way to achieve the overall goal. The challenge for the manager is to know which are the right battles.

Know your problem

This was my big break. I got to present to the CEO. I gave what I thought was a brilliant presentation. At the end of it the CEO coughed quietly and seemed to confirm my judgement of my own talents.

'That was a very impressive presentation' he said 'I only have one question. . .'

I was ready for any question. I had 200 back-up pages of detailed analysis. This was my chance to shine.

'What, precisely, was the problem you were solving?' he asked.

That was the one question I was not ready for. I quickly vanished into a puff of my own vanity and confusion.

---

2 Focus on causes, not symptoms

No one would think of trying to cure chicken pox by using spot remover. But such confusion over symptoms and causes happens regularly in business. Many cost-cutting programmes fall into this trap. The CEO looks strong and effective announcing some target job cuts or cost savings. In highly macho form the message was conveyed to the CEO's management team as: 'Give me 20 per cent cost reduction and 20 per cent head count in 12 months, or you will be part of the 20 per cent. No exceptions for units which are growing, which have already made cost gains or which are already best in class compared to peers. 20 per cent: read my lips.' Over 15 per cent was delivered and some top executives were fired. It took years for the business to recover from the mindless cost cutting of marketing (loss of market position and revenues) of R&D (loss of new product flow) and of talent (loss of morale).

Cost problems are always a symptom of something else, such as:

- inadequate revenues, which in turn may be a product problem, marketing and sales problem, distribution problem
- wrong product and customer mix, which are expensive to serve and do not pay enough to justify the cost
- ineffective processes and inefficient working practices.

The business goes in dramatically different directions if you choose to focus on increasing revenues, changing the product and customer mix or improving processes and working practices. Simple head count reduction will not achieve any of these positive outcomes.

At a smaller scale, many HR practices deal with symptoms, not causes. Performance-based appraisal and promotion systems sound highly dynamic. But they focus on symptoms (how well did the person do?) versus causes. Understanding the causes of good or poor performance is at least as important as measuring the outcome:

- Why did they do well or poorly?
- What skills need to grow to raise performance?
- What assignments will best suit this person in future?
- Are they building the right skills and experiences for their career and promotion prospects?
- How can performance be improved?

The skills-based approach to appraisal results in a better appraisal discussion. The good/bad performance appraisal can be confrontational and not very actionable. Many managers shy away from giving bad news, which helps no one. Focusing on causes (not skills) is more positive and actionable.

Anyone can spot a symptom of a problem. It does not take a genius to see that profits are not high enough. The mark of a good manager is one who can go beyond symptoms and unearth the root causes of the problem. There are no easy short cuts available. But there is one simple principle – keep on asking one question: 'Why?'

3 Prioritise the problems

Management is never short of problems and challenges. There are not enough hours in the day to solve them all. So managers have to be selective. Three simple questions help identify which problems are worth addressing:

1   *Is it important?* Does this problem make a significant difference to achieving my overall goals? Put it another way, if this problem is not resolved will it have a serious adverse effect? Is there a simple stop-gap solution which will prevent things getting worse while I concentrate on other problems?

2   *Is it urgent?* Do today what you have to do today. Will the problem be worse tomorrow than it is today, and does it matter? If it does, act now. Can I buy time? Problems do not always become worse: time has a habit of throwing up more information, more opportunities and more potential solutions. It can also heal emotional upsets.

3   *Is it actionable?* One of the dubious joys of management is to have to live with problems which you can do little or nothing about. You may be at the mercy of strategic challenges and decisions, IT projects going awry or competitive pressures forcing sudden and unexpected demands on you. Under these circumstances, the best thing to do is nothing. Do not worry about things you cannot control or influence. Be clear about who has responsibility for what.

Problem-solving tools

Most managers solve most problems intuitively. It is rare that managers sit down and do a formal problem analysis. But it helps to have a few tools and techniques at hand. You do not need to get pen and paper out every time you want to use them. It is enough to have the frameworks in your mind, and then you can use the framework to check and challenge your own thinking.

Here, we cover six classic problem-solving aides:

1   Cost–benefit analysis

2   SWOT analysis

3   Field force analysis

4   Multifactor/trade-off/grid analysis

5   Fishbone/mind maps

6   Creative problem solving.

All of these approaches have value in different contexts. The key is to pick the right approach for the right context. Typical assumptions for each approach are:

1   Cost–benefit analysis. Assumes a well-defined problem and solution which needs to be evaluated financially for formal approval.

2   SWOT analysis. Assumes a highly ambiguous, often strategic, challenge which needs further structuring.

3   Field force analysis. Assumes a choice is to be made between two courses of action including non-financial and qualitative criteria.

4   Multifactor/trade-off/grid analysis. Assumes a choice between multiple competing options with multiple criteria of varying importance.

5   Fishbone/mind maps. Assumes that there is a problem where the root causes need to be identified and which needs to be broken down into bite-sized chunks.

6   Creative problem solving. Assumes a highly complex problem to which there is no known answer and an original approach is required.

1 Cost–benefit analysis

This is the staple of all good management decision making. When it is not used, disaster often ensues. The disciplines of cost–benefit analysis are most commonly abused on IT system changes which are sold in on the basis of being 'strategic'. The problem is compounded in the public sector where it is difficult to identify any financial benefits. Fiascos in public sector IT procurement are regular: the NHS, tax credit system, Child Support Agency are a few UK examples.

A strong cost–benefit analysis is highly compelling. It forces management to take a proposal seriously: no executive wants to turn down a credible proposal which is financially attractive. The key here is credibility. It is not enough to produce a financially attractive proposal. It has to be credible. There are three elements to making the proposal credible:

1 Strong, logical reasoning.

2 Validation of the numbers by the finance department: if it does not support the calculations, then you are dead meat. Involve finance early, get its advice and buy in. Make sure you produce numbers to a format that finance recognise and can approve.

3 Operational credibility. Venture capitalists look beyond the numbers to the people who are behind the numbers. They back people as much as they back ideas. Executives do the same. It pays to find highly credible supporters and backers for your proposal. Investment proposals are as much political exercises as they are intellectual exercises: PQ and IQ work hand in hand.

Each organisation will have its own way of looking at financial benefits. The most common are:

▶ payback period

▶ ROI (return on investment)

▶ NPV (net present value).

Of these three, payback is the simplest but NPV is the most rigorous and is relatively easy. ROI is only included because it is widely used: in its simple form it is misleading and in its more refined form it is very complicated.

Payback period

How long will it take me to recoup my investment? One bank has a three-year payback period for staff redundancies. If it costs $100,000 to fire someone who costs the bank $50,000 a year including benefits, then the payback period is two years and it passes the three-year test, provided no replacement is hired.

Return on investment

This is where things get sticky. There are many different ways of calculating ROI. Each expert will start climbing the wall and spitting blood if you do not use their pet method. So the advice is to work with your finance department and discover which rules they play to. Enlist its support and, preferably, get it to do the calculation for you.

The problems start by knowing what the required rate of return should be. There are long, learned and tedious debates about this which involve discussion of forecast and historic equity risk premiums, and one versus five year betas, and much more. We will avoid that debate for now. For most managers, the required ROI is mandated from above. It may vary according to the risk of the project: a cost-savings programme may have a required return of 10 per cent, expansion into a new market may have a required return of 15 per cent to adjust for the risk of the project. To do this analysis you need to know the cost of the investment and the net benefits it will produce over its lifetime, together with whatever rate of return you are required to achieve. A simple worked example, looking at the cost of installing AVR (automatic voice response) in a call centre to replace humans, follows.

Worked example

The cost of the AVR machine is $1,000 today. It will cost $100 a year to maintain, but it will save $500 of labour, so the net annual benefit is $400. At the end of four years, it will be given away to charity: it will have no resale value.

The ROI calculation now looks like this:

(a) Required return: 15 per cent

(b) Year	0	1	2	3	4	Total
(c) Investment ($)	−1000					−1000
(d) Net benefits ($)		400	400	400	400	+1600

The simplest form of ROI is as follows: [(Total benefits − total costs)/total costs] × (100/number of years). In this case, the calculation would be:

$$ROI = [(1600 - 1000)/1000] \times 100/4 = 15\%.$$

This shows that this investment just meets the corporate goal of 15 per cent ROI.

This simple form of ROI is misleading. It assumes that a dollar today is worth as much as a dollar in four years' time: the next section shows this is untrue. The alternative to this form of ROI allows for the different value of a dollar over time. It is called IRR (internal rate of return) and is effectively the ROI on an investment which results in an NPV of zero. This requires first understanding NPV, which is useful.

The most practical solution is to work with whatever rules your finance department has in place. The rules may be wrong and misleading, but if that is how decisions are made, then it makes sense to work to those rules.

NPV: net present value

This is perhaps the most orthodox and reliable form of cost–benefit analysis.

The one key concept in here is the discount rate. This is a way of saying that a dollar today is worth more than a dollar tomorrow: I can invest today's dollar and make it worth $1.10 this time next year. And your promise of a dollar next year is much more risky than your offer of a dollar right now. Because of risk I will take less than one dollar (perhaps even 70 cents) right now instead of a promise of a dollar later. The discount rate adjusts for the time and risk effects of accepting a dollar later instead of a dollar now.

A 15 per cent discount rate implies that a dollar now is worth as much as a promise of $1.15 next year, $1.32 the year after and about $2 in five years' time. To put it the other way round: if I am promised $2 in five years' time, that is worth about $1 to me today. I apply a discount factor of 0.5 to the promise of a dollar in five years' time.

(a) Required return: 15 per cent						
(b) Year	0	1	2	3	4	Total
(c) Discount factor	1	0.87	0.76	0.66	0.57	
(d) Investment ($)	−1000					
(e) Cost savings ($)		400	400	400	400	
(f) Discounted cost/ benefit: (c) × ((d) + (e)) ($)	−1000	348	302	263	229	+144

This analysis also shows that the AVR is a worthwhile investment. But it is a very limited calculation because:

▶ It does not factor in major sensitivities and uncertainties (see below).

▶ It ignores second-order effects (disgruntled customers left hanging on the phone, and possibly switching supplier).

▶ It ignores alternatives (outsourcing or offshoring the call centre, upgrading the call centre to make it revenue generating through cross selling, segmenting the customers so that high-profit customers still get personal service, etc).

Sensitivity analysis

This gets us into the land of 'what if', for which spreadsheets are a saviour. 'What if' calculations allow us to test our major assumptions. For instance, in the NPV example above, the AVR project becomes unattractive (it achieves a negative NPV) if:

▶ the required return is raised to 20 per cent

▶ the AVR needs to be replaced after three years, not four

▶ the net cost savings turn out to be $300 per year, not $400

▶ the AVR kit costs $1200.

Managers quickly learn how to manipulate assumptions to ensure the right answer appears in the bottom right-hand corner of the spreadsheet.

In the most sophisticated world, different outcomes can be assigned different probabilities and a weighted NPV can be derived. Probability analysis is important is some industries: the profitability of financial leasing of computers depends heavily on resale values and likely depreciation rates; exploration for oil depends heavily on probabilities. But for most management decisions, decision making is much simpler. If a project only just scrapes past a cost–benefit analysis, it is probably not worth it: you know the numbers will have been fixed to pass the test and that reality is unlikely to be as rosy as the forecast. If a project is worthwhile, it tends to sail past any cost–benefit analysis with ease. If it underdelivers against forecast, it may still beat the required return for the organisation as a whole.

2 SWOT analysis

Not all problems succumb immediately to a cost–benefit analysis. Cost–benefit analysis implies a degree of certainty about outcomes. Managers know that the only true certainty is uncertainty. Putting some structure into ambiguous and uncertain situations helps decision making and problem solving. Perhaps the simplest way of structuring unstructured problems is a SWOT analysis. SWOT stands for:

Strengths

Weaknesses

Opportunities

Threats.

SWOT is a simple way of looking at strategic challenges. For instance, should Techmanics (a fictitious company) expand into China?

Strengths: Techmanics has some great technology and wonderful products which no one else can fully match. Strong R&D will keep them ahead of competition.

Weaknesses: No Chinese distribution, no Chinese staff who can understand the market.

Opportunities: Vast and growing market, especially in the luxury and gadget segment where Techmanics is focused. The high end of the market is highly profitable.

Threats. No intellectual property protection: Techmanics' products may be ripped off. Death Star Ventures may enter China before we do and condemn us to being also-rans.

This highly simplified SWOT analysis shows:

▶ The value of structuring a difficult challenge: it gives a framework for further discussion.

▶ The value of exploring alternative perspectives. In this case it looks at the costs and opportunities of expanding and *not* expanding into China, and at possible competitive reactions.

▶ The need to frame the issue before embarking on a detailed cost–benefit analysis.

3 Field force analysis

Field force analysis is a very fancy way of writing down the pros and cons, or the benefits and concerns of a specific decision. It is best used to evaluate a specific course of action where there are multiple, qualitative factors which affect the outcome. For instance, one company had a discussion about whether to introduce a floor cleaner based on a successful bathroom surface cleaner which already existed.

For the new product	Against the new product
Exploits an existing, trusted brand name	Might damage the existing brand
Uses spare factory capacity	Manufacturing complexity: changeover
Attacks competitor's profit sanctuary	Might lead to an expensive marketing war
Floor cleaners are a huge market	Expensive, risky to build market share
Our product is superior to competition	Competitor's products are well established
Our market tests went well	National conditions not the same as the test market

This simple analysis helps frame and focus the discussion. The 'Against' column becomes a risk and issue register. Standard problem-solving and brainstorming methods can be used to help resolve each of the risks and issues identified.

4 Trade-off/multifactor/grid analysis

This family of problem solving analyses is a good way of making a choice between multiple, hard-to-compare options. The real value of this approach is that it forces people to think about the criteria they are using to make a decision. It forces them to be explicit about how important one criterion is relative to another. This cuts through many rambling debates where managers are arguing for different choices and are using compelling but competing arguments. All the arguments cancel each other out and result in a tense stalemate. This approach prevents the stalemate and leads to a much more productive discussion.

The approach has six simple steps, which are often best taken in a group.

1   List the criteria for making the decision.

2   Score each criterion for how important it is.

3   List your options.

4   Score each option against each criterion.

5   Adjust the raw scores for the weightings you gave in step 2.

6   Add the scores up and, hopefully, come to an agreed outcome: if not, at least you will know why, and where you disagree you can have a more focused discussion.

The following example looks at the choice of a new office.

Choosing a new office

Start with the unweighted scores out of ten.

	Property			
Criterion	1	2	3	4
Ease of access for staff	9	3	6	7
Ease of access for customers	4	6	7	6
Cost	2	9	7	5
Length of lease	4	9	2	7
Layout of office	9	4	6	3
Prestige of building and address	9	2	6	4
Total	37	33	34	32

The first cut seems to show that property 1 is a clear winner. At this point, the CEO steps in and points out that just as all executives are not equal, so all criterion are not equal. The CEO assigns weightings to the criteria with the following results, where the unweighted scores have simply been multiplied by the weightings assigned by the CEO:

➤

Criterion (and CEO's weighting)	Property			
	1	2	3	4
Ease of access for staff (2)	18	6	12	14
Ease of access for customers (7)	28	42	49	42
Cost (10)	20	90	70	50
Length of lease (6)	24	54	12	42
Layout of office (5)	45	20	30	15
Prestige of building and address (4)	36	8	24	16
Total	171	220	197	179

The CEO is either fundamentally mean or is a diligent steward of share-holder's money. Either way, costs dominate the weightings, so that property 1 falls from being first choice to last and property 2 becomes a clear winner, even though layout and access for staff look highly unattractive.

5 Fishbone/mind maps

This family of problem-solving techniques is another area which has been hijacked by experts. These techniques are useful for breaking a big problem down into bite-sized chunks. They are also a good way of discovering the root cause of a problem, as opposed to its symptoms. They are very visual exercises, which are often best done in a small group setting. The experts are very particular about making you use different colours for different parts of your diagram and can inflict an entire philosophy on your simple need to solve a problem.

For our purposes, we can keep it simple. The key steps are:

1   State the problem (which appears as the head of the fish in the fish-bone).

2   Identify some of the major possible causes of the problem (the big bones of the fish).

3   Drill down in each major area and identify specific issues to address or investigate further (the small bones in the fish). You can drill down even further on any of these items, if necessary.

A simplified example of a fishbone analysis is shown here:

Fishbone diagram

As a result of this brainstorming, you will have identified the major causes of the problem/symptom. If there is agreement about the root cause, move to action. Otherwise, you may need to do some more legwork to understand individual issues. Either way, you will have broken a big and messy problem down into manageable chunks, and you will have moved away from dealing with symptoms to dealing with root causes. These are two valuable outcomes to achieve, especially if you do it in a group setting where you build buy-in and commitment to the way forward.

6 Creativity and creative problem solving

Not all problems can be solved by force of logic. The more interesting management challenges require a degree of creativity and invention. Asking managers to be creative will result in most of them breaking out in a cold sweat: creative workshops conjure up images of abysmal sessions where we all have to say what sort of tree/car/musician we would be if we were a tree/car/musician. Fortunately, there are some reliable ways of arriving at creative solutions without enduring the terminal embarrassment of a creativity workshop.

The simplest solution is to ask for help.

You may not know the solution, but others may. Even if they do not have the total solution, they can provide insights which may help you. There are plenty of exercises which demonstrate the power of the group to find a better solution than an individual can find. Desert, moon, space and island survival are all classic group dynamics exercises which prove the point. Type in 'desert survival' in any search engine and you will find plenty of helpful and free examples on the web.

The more formal solution is to ask for help in a structured way, through a problem-solving exercise. Here is a straightforward way to conduct the exercise in a series of steps:

1   Agree who is the problem owner and what the problem is you need to solve. Try to make the problem as specific and as focused as possible. Also, try to express it as an outcome. General and negative problems are difficult to solve, such as 'We are losing in the market.' Define the problem more closely and positively. 'How to increase retention rates among our most loyal customers' is going to lead to more actionable and positive solutions than the more general and negative version of the problem statement.

2   Outline the problem to a small group of people who between them have the knowledge, willingness and capability to provide insight and solutions. The ideal group has about four to seven people in it. Any fewer, and there are not enough to generate ideas and enthusiasm. Any more and it becomes chaotic.

3   Check for understanding of the problem statement, so that everyone is solving the same problem. Allow questions to check understanding, avoid any evaluation of the problem.

4   Generate ideas, and lots of them. Volume is good. Do not allow any evaluation of ideas at this stage. Get people to build on each other's ideas. Get people to look at the problem from different angles (competitors, customers, channels, costs, products, service, etc.) to stimulate more ideas. One person records the ideas onto a flipchart: this avoids too much duplication of ideas and lets contributors see that their ideas have been recognised so they do not feel the need to repeat

themselves. Make things move fast: make people state the headline of their idea only. As with any good newspaper headline, it should encapsulate the whole story. This makes it easier to record.

5   Select a few ideas to work on in detail. You can permit an outbreak of democracy at this stage. Give each person three votes, using Chicago rules. Chicago rules means that there are no rules: they can split their votes, sell their votes, steal votes or consolidate their votes. Do not get hung up on process. If two people had similar ideas, let them consolidate them into one: do not have a big debate, just let the owners of the two ideas decide if they want to merge. You will normally find that there is consensus around three to five workable ideas, and you will have done no evaluation of them so far.

6   Evaluate the most popular idea. Start by looking at why it is a good idea: evaluate its benefits. Managerial instinct is to look at problems first. The problem with problem focus is that it can kill good ideas. Once you understand why a problem is good, then you can start to explore some of the concerns it raises. Express the concerns in an action-focused manner: 'How to fund the idea' leads to action, whereas 'That is far too expensive' leads to conflict. How you state the concern leads to radically different outcomes.

7   If the solution you are all most excited about has some significant concerns attached, work through each of those concerns using the same process, starting at step 1 again. You will find yourself breaking the problem down into ever more manageable bite-sized chunks which you can deal with.

2.5 Strategic thinking: floors, romantics and the classics

If you listen to business school professors, strategy is so sophisticated and complicated that only they can really understand it. To prove their point, they come up with all sorts of clever concepts such as value innovation, strategic intent, core competences and co-creation. These are supported by matrices, grids and charts which give the appearance of analytical rigour.

Do not be deceived. Most strategic concepts are:

- ▶ selective rewriting of history of some successful companies
- ▶ better at describing the past than predicting the future
- ▶ based on a few simple truths.

Most corporate strategy is formulated the same way as most corporate budgets: last year's budget and strategy is the best predictor of next year's budget and strategy. Both will change, incrementally. But few companies actually change strategy significantly. The exceptions are famous, but exceptional. WPP, the world's largest advertising conglomerate was formed out of a shell company which made shopping trolleys. Nokia, the world's largest maker of mobile phones had its origins in rubber (largest shoe factory in Europe), plastics (floor coverings) and forestry products.

Because most businesses do not change strategy fundamentally, the demand for deep strategic thinking from managers is not high. Nevertheless, it helps to understand strategic thinking, so:

1 Understand the strategic relevance of your own activities

2 Know how to think strategically

3 Play the strategy game

4 Understand the nature of strategy.

If you can do these four things, you are well prepared for the executive suite.

1 Understand the strategic relevance of your own activities

I started to doubt the use of the word 'strategy' when the office manager started talking about strategic deployment of office space. I retired to the canteen to consider how I might strategically deploy my Brussel sprouts. As ever, the office manager was right and I was left to eat cold Brussel sprouts.

The office manager was answering the one strategic question which all managers have to be able to answer: 'How can my actions and decisions support the goals of the organisation?' At risk of stating the obvious, this requires more than simply understanding the goals you have been set in your annual plan: it requires understanding the goals of the senior leadership team. Many managers fail this obvious test: they are so consumed with meeting their immediate goals that they forget to think about the broader context in which they are operating.

The office manager had a strategic challenge all of his own. As we walked round the office we could see lots of consultants working in individual glass fish bowls: these were meant to combine privacy with open communication. In practice, the walls stopped communication and the glass prevented privacy. The manager had heard the CEO talk about the need for team work, transparency and focus on clients: that meant working at the client site, not in our cosy offices. The manager thought it through, and came up with a radically new design.

Out went all the mini-palaces which were also known as partners' offices. Instead, we were invited to share a common partners' room: we were being asked to walk the talk on team work. Quite a few partners exploded with indignant rage: they were the idle ones who would be most exposed in a common office. Next step were the consultants. Out went their goldfish bowls and their desks. In came rows of hot desks. There were not enough to go round, so consultants suddenly found it more congenial to work at the client site. In came lots of small meeting places so that teams could meet and work together.

The office manager had grasped the nature strategy well: he had understood the needs of the organisation and taken action to support those needs in his area. He had no need to understand grand corporate strategy, or to talk the language of core competencies. They were irrelevant. Managers do not need to be great strategists to think and act strategically: they need to understand the real needs of the organisation and to support those needs in their areas.

A simple test for strategic activity is this: will these actions get noticed at executive committee level? If they are relevant at that level, you are probably acting on matters which have strategic relevance. If not, you may still be making a useful but less visible contribution.

2 Know how to think strategically

The best strategic thinking is very simple. Clever people make things complicated. Really clever people make things simple. Many of the most successful organisations have very simple strategies:

▶ EasyJet and SouthWest Airlines: low-cost flying

▶ Dell: sell direct and make to order

▶ FedEx: overnight delivery, guaranteed.

Although they are very simple strategies, they are competitively devastating. Let us look at each in more detail to see why:

▶ EasyJet and SouthWest Airlines: low-cost flying. By starting with a zero cost base, and avoiding all the frills and complexity of full-service airlines, they achieved cost per mile and fares which the full-service airlines cannot reach with their legacy costs and infrastructure. They created clear competitive distance against the incumbents.

▶ Dell: sell direct and make to order. This eliminated all the sales forecasting problems, unsold stocks, cash-flow crises and fire sales that dogged the traditional model of selling through resellers. Incumbents felt unable to abandon their loyal resellers and were stuck.

▶ FedEx: overnight delivery, guaranteed. No one else did it at the time. Creating the nationwide infrastructure and building volume and scale fast made it hard for anyone to follow.

Now consider how much these strategies have changed over the past 20 years. Each organisation has essentially the same strategic formula as 20 years ago. Great strategies rarely change.

3 Play the strategy game

If you ever apply to join a strategy consulting firm, you will get a chance to play the strategy game, also known as the case method interview. It is worth practising this game: it gives insight into the prospects of your employer and enables you to hold your own in discussions with senior executives.

The ostensible purpose of the game is to find an answer to some imponderable business question such as: 'Should MegaBucks expand its product range from photography to other imaging products like copiers?' The real purpose of the game is to show that you can think in a structured and strategic manner: the actual answer is unimportant. Cynics might say that it is the essence of strategy consulting: show you are smart and do not worry too much about the answer.

To succeed, you do not need to know the right answer. You need to know the right questions. An effective strategy discussion will look at the issue from a series of different angles:

▶ What capabilities do we have? This gets at the core competence arguments of Hamel and Prahalad (management thinkers and academics). Imaging and photographic technology are close to each other, as Canon discovered by bridging both markets.

▶ What are the market prospects? Is it growing? Is it profitable? What are the pricing trends? Critically, you need to look at individual segments of the market. What segments are underserved? What needs are unmet? Canon identified that the old central copying function, focused on high volume, did not meet the needs of secretaries who needed just one or two quick copies locally. There was an unmet need for quick, cheap and average-quality copies. High speed was not important.

▶ What does the competition look like? Again, look for underserved market segments. Xerox was huge and looked unbeatable. But it had no product for distributed/local copying across the office.

▶ What are the economics of the market from a customer perspective? Instead of tying people into long leases for big copiers, secretaries would be happy to buy cheap local copiers.

▶ What are the economics from the manufacturer's perspective? The big money is in the replacement toner. This means the key is to get the copier onto the secretary's desk, if necessary at a loss, and then make money on the supplies. This then implies that the product must be simple to maintain and resupply, without the need for a technician. This in turn leads to a distribution model which is more mass market accessed via re-sellers than through the traditional model of B2B salesmen working on commission.

As you go through the game, you should keep in mind a checklist of questions and perspectives you need to cover:

- ▶ Capabilities.
- ▶ Market prospects, by segment: size, growth, profitability and cyclicality.
- ▶ Customer needs, by segment: remember product, price, positioning questions.
- ▶ Competitive position, by segment: What is our value proposition? Do we have any sustainable advantage, barriers to entry?
- ▶ Economics, relative to competition, the customer and ourselves. What are the effects of scale across the value chain? What is the value chain?

Keep asking these questions until you find convincing answers. Quite often you will find that just one critical insight develops out of all the questions. In the exotic world of wet cement supply, the economics of distribution favour the creation of a series of local monopolies. It takes some questioning to get to that simple outcome. Asking the set questions will quickly help you identify why Microsoft is highly profitable, whereas auto-manufacturing in mature economies is, at best, cyclical in terms of profitability.

4 Understanding the nature of strategy

It helps to know the language of strategy. Strategy is spoken in two very different languages: the classical and the postmodern.

Classical strategy

Classical strategy is a world of cause and effect. It is a search for the business equivalent of Newton's laws: 'If x happens, then y is the result.' It is strategy in the true tradition of the Enlightenment: finding universal rules to apply to all situations. The godfathers of this world are Michael Porter (Five Forces analysis) and the Boston Consulting Group (responsible for matrix mania). The good news is that these formulas shed light, and provide some insight, into complex situations.

The bad news about formulaic strategy is that it is extremely dangerous. If everyone uses the same tools and the same analysis, they come up with the same answers. This leads to the lemming syndrome: '10,000 lemmings cannot be wrong, so I will jump off a cliff as well. . .' The dot.com bomb was a classic lemming moment. UK telcos all did the same analysis and bid £22.4 billion for 3G licences: they are unlikely ever to get that money back. Smart bankers all decided that they needed to become market makers for UK government debt when the market was deregulated. The number of competitors rose from four to 26 which enabled them all to lose handsome amounts of money in what used to be a profitable market. Equally, going in the opposite direction of the formula can be highly profitable. Premier Foods makes it its business to buy up all the orphan brands being discarded by big food companies. The big food companies all do the same analysis which tells them to concentrate on big brands to gain scale economies and make money. Premier Foods is highly profitable, thank you very much.

Postmodern strategy

This is the language of a group of professors who all learned their trade from C.K. Prahalad (core competence, strategic intent). His acolytes include Gary Hamel, Chan Kim (value innovation) and Venkat Ramaswamy (co-creation). They are rebels against classical orthodoxy. For them, strategy is a process of discovery in which you create the future, rather than react to the present by analysing the past. This is a process-driven view of strategy much more than an analytical view of strategy. It does not pretend to have all the answers: it challenges organisations to discover and create answers for themselves.

The good news about this approach is that it leads to much more creative outcomes and engages the organisation more deeply. The problem is that the most famous cases these academics use (Canon, Cirque du Soleil, Honda) are all organisations which did not use their approach. The academics' approach has been retrofitted onto past experience. So the jury is still out as to whether they have created a process which leads to superior strategic outcomes.

Financial skills

Financial numeracy is a core skill for all managers. Unfortunately, financial skills are shrouded in unnecessary mystery. The high priests of accounting and finance cloak their art in terminology and techniques which are designed to scare off most managers. They are like medieval craft guilds who jealously protected their trade from all outsiders. Some areas of finance and accounting are genuinely complicated: understanding regulatory capital requirements for banks internationally is not the sort of area the average manager needs or wants to understand. But the core of financial and accounting skills should be core skills for all managers.

These skills are not purely intellectual skills. Most financial management skills are deeply political, because they involve allocation of resources, setting of targets, expectations and priorities. Inevitably, this goes to the heart of competitive strategy: how each department and each manager competes against the others to secure the right resources, expectations and targets. Formal financial tools are simply the weapons of choice for managers in these political and competitive battles. Only the most naïve managers accepts financial management as an objective, logical and rational exercise in which right and wrong answers can be discovered intellectually. The right financial solution is the one which best helps each manager to achieve their optimum goals.

The core financial skills required of all managers are explored in the following sections:

2.6 Setting budgets

2.7 Managing budgets

2.8 Managing costs

2.9 Surviving spreadsheets

2.10 Playing the numbers game

These are the main financial and political battle grounds for managers. Within each of these battle grounds there are accepted weapons, or analytical tools, which managers can use to achieve their goals. The nature of these weapons differs slightly by organisation. In any event, it is worth learning how to use these weapons to best advantage. Most traditional financial textbooks focus on finding the right answer and the right number. Managers do not use numbers in an intellectual pursuit of the ideal answer. Managers use numbers the same way lawyers use facts: they use facts and numbers selectively to support their case, not to illuminate the truth.

2.6 Setting budgets: the politics of performance

A budget is a contract between two levels of management: 'We agree to achieve the following in return for this much money.' As with all contracts, this is not a rational and objective exercise. It is a negotiation between the supplier of services (the less senior manager) and the buyer with the money (the more senior manager). Negotiation skills are covered fully in section 3.2. Unlike most negotiations, both the buyer and the seller in budget negotiations have roughly similar levels of information, they know each other's tactics and they know each other's styles. So the negotiation can become very intense.

Most budget negotiations have two major elements: anchoring and adjustment.

Anchoring the budget discussion

The best predictor of next year's budget is this year's budget. This year's budget is the anchor around which next year's budget will be negotiated. In many organisations, this is so well established that managers will fight hard to spend this year's budget fully and to not overachieve budget this year: underspending or overachieving simply leads to the budget anchor being reset. Next year's budget becomes much harder to achieve if you do too well this year (see the box on the next page). Such budget setting is clearly dysfunctional: it discourages performance improvement.

To effect real change, the anchor needs to be reset at a very different point from today. Anchoring needs to be achieved as early as possible, so that the debate is framed the right way. If the debate is framed around 'How far do we increase or decrease last year's budget?' only minor change will emerge. If the debate is anchored around 'Can we double our volume with just a 70 per cent increase in budget?' you have a radically different discussion. Anchoring determines the level of ambition for the organisation.

Anchoring needs to take place as part of the strategic planning process which should, in larger organisations, precede the annual budget cycle.

The best way to anchor a budget discussion is not by submitting a detailed strategic analysis to show why you should be targeting a doubling of sales volume. The best way is to talk very informally and very early on with the most senior people possible, before even the strategic planning process starts.

The coffee break anchor

Group CEO: 'Things look good this year. . .'

Business Unit Head (BUH): 'Next year could be even better. On current trends, 35 per cent growth is not impossible, if we have the resource to support it.'

CEO: '35 per cent? I thought we were on trend for nearer 20 per cent?'

BUH: '35 per cent assumes we invest in the new product stream that is coming on line. . .'

CEO: 'Sounds good, but cash flow will be a challenge. . .'

BUH: 'We'll look into it. . .'

Next year's budget discussion has just been anchored at 20–35 per cent growth, with the need to look at cash flow hard. Neither side has promised anything, yet. If this conversation had not happened, and instead the CEO had listened to the highly cautious CFO, the budget discussion could have been anchored around 10 per cent volume growth and a static budget.

Adjustments

Adjustments take the form of the question: 'What will be different next year from this year?' This is where there is intense negotiation on the detail. Adjustments look at incremental differences from this year: anchoring looks at step-change differences from this year. Typical incremental differences will include:

- productivity improvements
- inflation, salaries, etc.
- new initiatives and projects
- market and competitive trends
- pricing opportunities and pressures.

These discussions can be like trench warfare. Staff functions tend to have the advantage in these discussions because they:

- have the support and power of senior management on whose behalf they are acting
- are working 100 per cent on budget discussions, while managers have to manage a business as well.

Consequently, many managers give up too easily. This is a mistake. It is better to have one nightmare month of negotiating a budget you can achieve than to spend one year working to deliver a budget which was set too high.

This debate is reversed from senior management's perspective. They know that there will be widespread game playing in the budget negotiations, with each budgetholder having well-rehearsed arguments as to why the outlook is uniquely grim for the future and delivering any sort of profit will be nearly impossible. There are two defences against this for senior managers:

1   Staff warfare: use the staff in planning and finance to run the process, challenge and check facts, and maintain a semblance of honesty in the debate.

2   Be selectively unreasonable. Good managers are selectively unreasonable. Reasonable managers listen to all the excuses as to why something is not possible. Any reasonable manager would have told Kennedy that his dream of putting a man on the moon within ten years was not possible: the technology, skills, organisation and money simply did not exist. Reasonable managers would have been right in their assessment, and that is why they have been forgotten. Unreasonable managers demand outstanding performance and then support and enable it. Turning a deaf ear to excuses is a useful skill, even if it irritates the managers who are doing the special pleading.

2.7 Managing budgets: the annual dance routine

Each year follows a predictable budget cycle. The year starts full of hope. Then there is a gradual squeeze over the year. High-performing units suddenly have their goals raised even higher to make up for the shortfall in the weaker units. Weaker units start to get more help than they care for: being behind budget is an uncomfortable experience. This cycle shapes the way managers need to manage their budget.

▶ *Know your numbers in advance of the official data.* The purpose of this is to show that you are in control of the operation, and to take early corrective action if things are going off course. By the time you receive the report saying that your budget has crashed, it is too late. Accounting data looks backwards: you cannot drive the business forwards by looking backwards. Most departments should be able to predict three months in advance what will be happening: sales will have a sales pipeline, HR will have a recruiting pipeline. Significant challenges with competitor activity, customers running into payment problems or major projects overrunning should be visible to a manager who is in control. Use this sort of information to create your own early-warning radar system.

▶ *Prepare for a rainy day.* Two simple principles help here:

1 The 48/52 rule is a simple discipline which calls for spending 48 per cent of your budget but achieving 52 per cent of your goals in the first six months of the financial year. This builds up some reserve for things going wrong later in the year. Even if things go wrong in the first half, the 48/52 rule means that your first half outcome might still be close to 50/50.

2 Sandbag. You should have constructed your original budget so that you know were there is fat to be cut: maybe you know there is a supplier who can be squeezed further, or a project cost has been overestimated, or a marketing campaign is a little too rich. As you go through the year, you can quietly stash some of these savings away for later.

▶ *Manage communications well.* There are three principles here:

1 Avoid surprises. If there is bad budget news looming, prepare the way early and let top management know in advance the challenge, and its cause and your proposed solution. Stay in control. If they call you asking you to explain a negative variance, you have a problem. You look like you were not in control, you are on the defensive and you are about to get the sort of staff and senior management help that no sane manager wants.

2 Avoid boasting. It is human nature to brag when thing are going well. It is senior management's nature to revise your budget upwards if they see things are going well. If things are going well, reset expectations low: show that the second half of the year will be much more challenging than the first half. Keep your original budget commitment for as long as possible.

3 Don't whine, negotiate. If your budget revision is mandated from the top, use it to renegotiate your commitments. Do not offer something for nothing.

▶ *Prioritise your spending.* Phase spending carefully. There is a delicate balance to be achieved here. The reserving principle requires delaying expenditure. But the knowledge that budgets will become tighter later in the year requires bringing some spending forward. The spending to bring forward is a mixture of two elements:

1 Essential investments for the business which may get cut later in the year. Productivity investments which take time to pay back are vulnerable to a year-end squeeze.

2 Discretionary spending which will certainly be cut in any squeeze, but which you need to build your team and its skills. Items such as conferences, training courses and laptop replacements are very easy to cut: if you believe they are important for any reason, spend the money before it is taken away.

All of these disciplines assume that you have accurate financial data. Perhaps the fastest way to lose credibility with an executive team is to produce unreliable data. If it cannot trust your data, it cannot trust you. It pays to have a good accountant on your team who can provide the information and the cover you need.

Budget utility and futility

Aged 18, I managed to find ten weeks' work at the Inland Revenue. It was the employer of last resort and I was the employee of last resort. We were the perfect match.

The work itself was an education in futility. I had to alter, by hand, the tax codings of 10,000 taxpayers. This meant adding three numbers together to create a fourth number. The inefficiency was staggering:

▶ ten weeks work took five weeks, at most

▶ the work could have been done in seconds by a computer

▶ the work was irrelevant anyway because the day after this annual ritual was completed, the government would again change the tax codings and the work would have to start all over.

In week eight my manager was in a great flap. He wanted me to do something, anything, to look busy. An inspector was coming and if he saw that I had already finished the ten weeks task, he might conclude that ten weeks was too long. As a result the manager's budget would be cut for the next year. So I looked busy, the manager kept his budget and I was given a pint of beer after work. Everyone was happy, except the long-suffering taxpayer: nothing new there, then.

I was starting to suspect that business and budgets were not all about efficiency and rationality. Politics and power seemed to be involved. But I assured myself that this was just the Inland Revenue. What else could you expect of a monopoly enforced by government? Surely other businesses and budgets would be far more rational and efficient with no hint of politics, wouldn't they?

2.8 Managing costs: minimising pain

Managing costs is at the heart of the management task. Inevitably, managers are squeezed. Input costs always go up: customers rarely volunteer price rises, staff rarely volunteer salary cuts, suppliers always want more and the tax inspector is always happy to steal another penny or two. On the other hand, there is the relentless logic of senior management and of the marketplace which demands betterfastercheaper: don't just cut costs, but do things better as well. People no longer accept a cost–quality trade off. They want both.

This pressure builds up like clockwork towards the financial year end. The year starts full of hope. As the year progresses, achieving targets becomes ever-more challenging. One product or region hits a big problem, so the pain gets shared around the organisation: every other region and product has their goals raised to make up for the shortfall in the Japanese widgets market, the safety recall in Europe or the litigation in the USA.

By year end, management inevitably are looking at key ratios for the annual report. So expect the following demands:

▶ Cut costs, to make our EPS (earnings per share) target. Cutting costs is easier, faster and more certain than raising revenues. And it feeds straight to the bottom line. It also creates problems for next year, but we will worry about next year, next year.

▶ Manage cash by squeezing suppliers (pay late) and customers (demand payment now).

▶ Get creative: capitalise expenditure, make some more exceptional provisions, delay major projects, recognise revenues as early as possible.

The astute manager knows that this squeeze is coming, and will prepare for it. That preparation comes in the form of a five-fold defensive strategy, outlined below. The purpose of cost cutting when it is part of the budget cycle is to do the minimum required to deliver the arbitrary demands of senior management and to avoid doing any substantive damage to the business itself. Short-term, budget-driven cost cuts are fundamentally different from the planned productivity improvements which all managers should seek anyway. Productivity is about real cost improvements; budget cost cuts involve considerable game playing by all levels of management. The five levels of defence against the budget-driven cost-cutting demands are:

1   Play the game

2   Soft squeeze

3   Hard squeeze

4   Real change

5   Pretend to make real change.

1 Play the game

Managers have three major tools to play with here. Each one of them is designed to avoid making any serious cost cuts which would harm the business.

1   *Sandbagging*. This is the gentle art of keeping as much in reserve and hidden from the prying eyes of management and staff for as long as possible. There is little point in squeezing suppliers mid-year: there will be nothing left to squeeze when top management insist on everyone delivering the 20 per cent improvement in payables and receivables by year end. This edict will inevitably punish the well-managed unit, while leaving the more politically astute unit with no real problems.

2   *KKK*: this is the Japanese alliteration for consultants, advertising and entertaining. In Japan, they are generally considered easy and harmless things to cut. Each country and organisation will have its equivalent of KKK: it might be consultants, conferences and training elsewhere. Naturally, if you have a conference you are really committed to, make sure it is booked, paid for and non-refundable before the squeeze edict is issued.

3   *Timing*. Be prepared to delay costs or accelerate revenues. If you are having a really good year, work hard to accelerate costs and defer revenues: if you overachieve this year, you will simply have a higher target next year. Better to start next year with a modest target but a very fast start in performance terms.

This game has to be played the right way. There are two common mistakes made when taking part:

1   Conceding to the new target too easily.

2   Whining about the new target. Telling management that it will be really hard to meet the target will make it feel good: you have just confirmed that you can meet the new target with hard work. Management likes managers to work hard and meet targets.

If you can, use the new target as an opportunity to negotiate. This is a way of making management understand that cutting costs has consequences, and it needs to deal with them. Cost cuts cannot be imagined out of thin air. There are two things you can try to ask for:

1   A delay in achieving a tough project which is close to the heart of management: this will test management resolve and give you more time to deliver. The excuse, of course, is that less budget means less support so more time is needed for completion.

2   A downwards revision in the goals for next year: underinvesting now has performance consequences later.

Your success in renegotiating requires persistence, eloquence, political support and some luck. But if you don't ask the question, you don't get the answer.

2 The soft squeeze

Once the game playing is over, managers may have to deliver some real cost cuts. This soft squeeze goes through four levels of pain:

1   Squeeze discretionary external staff and costs: look hard at temporary, contract and consulting staff. If necessary, show them the same level of loyalty that most of them have for you. Get rid of them.

2   Squeeze internal discretionary staff: stop overtime.

3   Put in a headcount freeze. This normally requires making it very hard to hire replacement staff when someone leaves: you still need to find ways of putting extra staff into areas where they are most needed. So if someone leaves, do not assume they can automatically be replaced: the effort of that head may be better used elsewhere.

4   Put in a hiring freeze. This now starts to cause pain. No leaving staff are replaced. Often the areas under the most pressure have the highest staff turnover, so a headcount freeze hurts most where you can least afford it. Reassigning staff is often difficult because the skills mix is not right. It is tough to sustain a hiring freeze, except for very short periods. Even at this stage, a manager will have kept as much of the team together as possible. Cutting the team is bad for morale and leaves the operation weakened.

3 The hard squeeze

This is where the pain really starts. The last ditch of defence is voluntary redundancy which can be achieved in two ways:

1   *Raising the bar*. Raise the performance bar, and quietly counsel the lower performers out. This is an elegant solution which may increase the overall quality of the team and gets rid of people who have not been contributing enough. The problem is that this needs time: time to establish the performance track record (or lack of it) and time to ease people out. It works as a long-term management practice, but is difficult in response to a short-term cost-cutting drive.

2   *Asking for volunteers*. This tends to be a disaster. It is an admission that the ship is sinking, so the people who can swim will swim. The best people who can get jobs elsewhere will go. Anyone who cannot get a job elsewhere clings desperately to the sinking ship. This is precisely not the team you want to keep.

The final alternative is to make involuntary redundancies. This is clearly an organisation in some crisis. There is no kind way of firing people. As with executions, there are less cruel ways: doing it fast is better than spinning out the agony for the victims. Let the unlucky people go with as much of their dignity intact as possible, and with as much hope for the future as possible. But the big trap is to focus too much on them. This sounds cruel, but managers are going to have to live and work with the survivors, not the losers. It makes sense to invest as much time as possible in helping the survivors see that there is still hope, there is still a future and that they can be part of it.

4 Making real change

None of the cost-cutting efforts described above actually improve the underlying performance of the business. Knee-jerk cost cuts look impressive and help the CEO get a bigger bonus. But they do not help the business.

In practice, real change comes from two different angles:

1   Steady operational improvement: the *kaizen* approach of improving

costs and quality a few per cent each year. Reducing costs by 4 per cent annually achieves more and is less painful than the once in five years, macho 20 per cent cost-cutting campaign.

2   Strategic change. This is about making structural change to the cost model: eliminating unprofitable and high-cost products, markets and channels; developing new technologies, products and markets; changing the competitive position. All of this looks very easy when written in a report but is very difficult to achieve.

The problem with all the real changes is that all your competitors are doing more or less the same with roughly as much skill and talent as you are. Each year you run harder and harder simply to stay still compared to competition. At least no one pretends that management is easy.

5 Pretend to make real change

The need to make continual cost and productivity improvements is real. Even the most successful organisations cannot stand still. But the more successful an organisation is, the less managers will feel the need to make painful decisions. Inevitably, therefore, they will find ways of showing that they are making great improvements while in reality they are achieving nothing. This sort of cost cutting delivers red dollars: they look great but have no value compared to green dollars. There are two basic ways of delivering red dollars:

1   *Squeeze the balloon.* Squeezing a balloon pushes air from one part of the balloon to another, it does not reduce the amount of air in it. Squeezing the corporate balloon transfers costs from one place to another to create a mirage of improvement. There are two ways of squeezing the balloon:

   (a) Transfer costs to other departments: increase transfer prices, charge for previously free services (IT help desks, legal support, payroll administration, etc.).

   (b) Transfer costs to another year: delay paying customers, delay major expenditures, capitalise costs (then pay depreciation of the new-found assets over the next five years).

2   *Scoreboarding.* This is a favourite of consultants and project managers who have to show results from their project. Again, there are two basic ways of scoreboarding:

(a) Count all the potential gains as real gains: the reengineering project may have identified 20 per cent excess capacity across 50 people. But you cannot cut 20 per cent of each person. So the project leader agrees with the line manager that a 20 per cent (or ten staff) cost reduction has been identified and then adds the 20 per cent to the long list of cost savings the project has achieved. With tedious regularity, senior management fail to follow up and check that the 20 per cent has actually been delivered by the line manager.

(b) Changing the baseline. If a department is looking for a 30 per cent increase in budget and then settles for a 15 per cent increase, be ready for the claim that it has cut its budget by 15 per cent. A 15 per cent increase has been converted into a 15 per cent cut. This ploy is greatly favoured by politicians when debating budgets.

Game playing like this is a sure sign of a fat and bloated organisation. Knowing how the games are played can help you spot and control them, or to play them, as conditions require.

The mysterious case of the missing $35 million

Head office calmly announced it was increasing its budget from an already outrageous $94 million to $134 million. That was $40 million of potential bonus money which it was stealing. When challenged on the number, it threw down a challenge: 'If anyone thinks they can reduce this very tough budget to less than $100 million, they are welcome to try.' Head office managers smirked, knowing that no one is dumb enough to make enemies of the whole of head office.

Well, more or less no one is that dumb. Unfortunately for them and for me, I was in the room. I volunteered for career suicide. The challenge was to find $35 million of apparent savings without creating mortal enemies of every powerful panjandrum in the business. Follow the red dollar dance:

> ▶ Use the wrong baseline: cutting a notional budget of $134 million is far easier than cutting real spending and real jobs from this year's budget of $94 million. I could 'cut' $35 million and still leave head office with an increase in budget of over 5 per cent ($94 million to $99 million).
>
> ▶ Transfer costs: head office loved this. We started charging for everything, even the voicemail system. Out went the 0800 number, in came a regular toll number. The business was no better off in total, but head office was able to show a reduction in its net cost.
>
> ▶ Capitalise as many costs as possible: move head office to a site where we owned the freehold, and forget to charge rent. Huge apparent savings in expenditure. Extend the laptop replacement cycle from two years to four years.
>
> The exercise officially saved $35 million. In practice it achieved zero cost savings for the business. But it did save my career, so it was a very worthwhile exercise.

2.9 Surviving spreadsheets: assumptions, not maths

In the bad old days, before spreadsheets, junior managers could impress by producing data sheets where all the columns and rows added up and there were no rounding errors. Senior managers showed off by doing some quick mental arithmetic to show that not all the rows and columns added up correctly. Then everyone would have 40 minutes of forensic fun figuring out where the maths went wrong. There was a naïve assumption that good maths equalled good thinking and dodgy maths equalled dodgy thinking.

In the spreadsheet era, we do not have to worry about dodgy maths so much, unless someone is using elaborate equations. Spreadsheets should allow managers to focus much more on the thinking, not on the maths. In practice, the spreadsheet assumes a life of its own. The person producing the spreadsheet deploys two basic tactics:

1   Start at the bottom right-hand corner. You know the answer must be *x*% or $*y* million. So keep on adjusting the spreadsheet inputs until *x* or *y* is achieved. Then add a safety margin and make sure the number does not look suspiciously round.

2   Overwhelm the opposition (senior managers and staffers) with data. About 200 lines and 40 columns of data over six interrelated pages should scare off most people, especially when all they really want to see is whether the number in the bottom right-hand corner of the spreadsheet looks good: *x* or *y* with a bit of safety margin built in.

The standard defence against this continues in the tradition of the bad old days: search for the dodgy number. The easiest way to do this is to look at the detail. This becomes a trivia hunt. The big numbers are too big and complicated, but everyone knows that allowing an average of $15 per cup of coffee is absurd. So if that appears in the spreadsheet, everyone gets to play the game of 40 minutes forensic fun searching out more dodgy trivia.

The rules for the spreadsheet survival game are very simple, and are completely different if you are writing the spreadsheet or reading it.

The spreadsheet writer should:

▶ Start with the desired answer in the bottom right-hand corner.

▶ Work out whatever scenarios and assumptions justify getting to the answer.

▶ Make minor but easily checked assumptions very conservative so that you appear not to be reckless and have evidence to show you are careful.

▶ Cover your tracks: leave some safety margin and avoid round numbers.

▶ Get key people to validate the key assumptions in your model, so that senior management cannot pick it apart. Validation is the most painful, but useful, part of the exercise: it is employed in the process of checking assumptions with sales, marketing, HR, finance and other relevant experts to gain insight, test thinking and build credibility for later.

For the spreadsheet reader, the rules are largely reversed.

▶ Ignore the answer, unless it is not what you want to see. Assume it has been fudged.

▶ Before you look at the spreadsheet, think of the five major assumptions that will drive the outcome, and note what 'reasonable' might look like for each assumption.

▶ Before you look at the spreadsheet, ask the spreadsheet writer what assumptions he or she has made for the five major drivers you have identified. You may well have a lively discussion at this point.

▶ Ask 'what if. . .' questions: What if each of the major assumptions lands up being different from what you are expecting? Where are the risks? How can you mitigate those risks?

▶ Only now is it worth actually looking at the spreadsheet.

2.10 Knowing numbers: playing the numbers game

Numbers make many people feel nervous. With a degree in history, numbers certainly made me feel nervous. I was not even much good at dates. The critical breakthrough came in discovering that management numbers are not about maths: they are about thinking and persuasion. Even historians can manage that, on a good day. In contrast, not all mathematicians feel confident about business thinking and persuasion. The numbers game is an equal opportunity challenge for all disciplines: it is equally tough for everyone.

There are four major variations of the numbers game:

1   The assumptions game
2   The averages game
3   The baseline game
4   The validation game.

1 The assumptions game

This is how to look smart whenever presented with a complex spreadsheet or proposal. Do not worry about the maths. Look at the largest figures and then test the assumptions behind them. This has been covered fully in spreadsheet survival above. Typical assumptions to test involve:

- the market: size, growth, share
- customers: number, cost to acquire, cost to serve, attrition
- operations: cost per job, overhead per person, property, systems
- people: number required, cost per person, cost to hire, attrition.

The way to succeed at this game is to create your own checklist of assumptions before you even see the spreadsheet or proposal. Do not get caught up in the Byzantine internal logic of the proposal in front of you. Make sure your own thinking and assumptions are clear, then it becomes easy to test other people's thinking and assumptions.

2 The averages game

Averages are profoundly misleading. The human population is on average 51 per cent female. Useless. Average customer satisfaction is 3.2 on a five-point scale. Utterly useless. Of far more use to a manager are the extremes and the segments, for example:

- If average customer satisfaction is 3.2, how many are really happy and how many really unhappy with us? Why? How many of the unhappy ones leave us? How can we make the happy ones even more happy? Does average satisfaction cover up delight with one thing we do (in-store service) and disgust with another (telephone support)?
- The average (possibly median or mean, but we will let that distinction pass) household income is $58,000 in the USA. So what? Does this mean that there is no market for private jets or upmarket hotels and holidays?
- The average temperature of someone with their head in the oven and their feet in the freezer is probably quite acceptable. Do not try this experiment at home (or elsewhere).

When faced with an average, always look for the extreme scores behind the average, and the major segments around the average: that is where the real insight will come from.

Sneezing at averages

The car was full of a new toilet soap which we were going to launch nation-ally. It had an overpowering fragrance, which made everyone in the car sneeze. After four hours of driving and sneezing, we hated it as much as the consumers in our market research. And we were its managers. We wondered how a toilet soap which scored so low in research could go national. The answer was that in the test market, it had done very well. This made the riddle even more confusing.

The market research was based on all consumers, most of whom hated it even if they were not sneezing at it. But about 15 per cent of the population thought it was brilliant, the best toilet soap they had ever tried. Given that no toilet soap had more than 10 per cent of the market, this was extremely good news. Following the market research, we put the soap into test market and the 15 per cent of die hards duly bought the soap in vast quantity and at great expense.

The average reaction to our product was irrelevant. We had a profitable hit on our hands, based on one segment of the market. Now all we had to do was to sneeze our way to the national sales conference. . . .

---

3 The baseline game

Beating baselines is a classic intellectual and political challenge for managers. Setting a baseline ought to be a rational and objective exercise. It is not. It is a political exercise which fundamentally affects perceptions of performance. Naïve managers ignore this and accept given baselines: experienced managers understand that the right performance baseline makes beating the baseline much easier than accepting a challenging baseline.

The two key variations of this game are:

1   The declining baseline
2   The false baseline

1 The declining baseline

A baseline is perhaps the most deceptive and dangerous assumption in business. It is deceptive because it seems so natural and reasonable, and it is dangerous because it is often wrong. Spot what is wrong in these two cases.

▶ *Case one*: Our current budget is $15 million a year. We have worked very hard and we have identified cost savings of 15 per cent. Even allowing for 5 per cent inflation, that means we can deliver about 10 per cent cost savings. That means $1.5 million for the bottom line. Can I have my bonus please?

▶ *Case two*. Our market share is 10 per cent. We have decided to reinvest the cost savings from case one into a major price reduction. We know from market research and from a small test market we did, that a 10 per cent price reduction in this price-sensitive market will have a dramatic effect and we will increase our market share to 15 per cent. This is such a scale sensitive business, that growth will be highly profitable.

The fallacy in both cases is to assume that the baseline is stable over time. The starting point of the current budget or market position is never stable over time. In business, all such baselines are on a continual downwards trend. Competitors wreck our plans by improving their efficiency and cutting costs as well. Competitors will match our efforts in both case one and case two: we will make the cost savings as promised, but there will be no increase in profit or market share as long as competition do as well as we can. We are running hard to stay still.

Even without the effect of competition, organisations still face a declining baseline. Every organisation slowly slides towards chaos: experienced staff leave and new staff come in who need training; suppliers mess up; customer demands change; technology makes our current ways of working redundant; machines and systems break down; events happen. Against this background, huge effort is required simply to keep things in a steady state. The consequences of this are significant:

▶ Cost-savings programmes rarely result in profit improvements: all the savings get competed away by equally vigorous competitors. Only customers gain from your efforts.

▶ Sales and marketing programmes struggle to build market share, given the effects of competition.

▶ Managers have to run hard to stay still: doing as well as last year takes enormous effort to cope with the adverse effects of competition and the internal forces of entropy which work against success.

2 The false baseline

The false baseline is used by managers at all levels, and in particular by CEOs. It is the natural, political response to the problem of the declining baseline. The purpose of the false baseline is to set the starting point so low, that anything you do has to be an improvement on where you are today.

When you inherit a job, you may well find that the person who preceded you has left a picture of a great job brilliantly done, which is why they were promoted. They will have shown that they had put in place all the plans required to transform the business. If you allow that propaganda to flourish, you are dead meat. If you succeed, it will be because of the plans that the previous incumbent put in place. If you do less than brilliantly, it will be because you messed up. You do not want to inherit a baseline set impossibly high.

The alternative is to show, as fast as possible, that the job or department you inherited is on the brink of collapse. Everything is a disaster which only a superhero can possibly turn around, but luckily you have arrived in the nick of time. If things now proceed modestly well, you will have done a great job in averting disaster.

The same modest performance can be seen as a disaster or as a triumph, depending on how the baseline was set.

4 The validation game: cowboys, sheriffs and mayors

The validation game is about people and politics as much as it is about numbers. Venture capitalists, bankers and senior managers do not simply look at the numbers being presented to them. They look at the people behind the numbers. A solid proposal from a team with high credibility is more convincing than an exciting proposal from a weak team.

Effective managers understand this and will use it to their advantage. Validation is required from two sources. First, get the sheriff and his deputies on board. You can find them in marketing, HR, IT, finance and accounting. They will all want their say. Let them have it, in private. Let them nitpick in private. The important thing is to get them on your side. Once you have the sheriff on board, approach the mayor. The mayor is the local power broker.

Whereas the sheriff and deputies are interested in the detail of their individual areas, the mayor is interested in the bigger picture: how your numbers fit with all the other priorities and numbers in town.

Once you have lined up the sheriff, deputies and mayor to support you, you can really go to town and have fun. The other cowboys will not even get a look in.

3

EQ skills:

dealing with people

Fortunately, you do not have to be a certified tree hugger to have good EQ skills. EQ is not about being nice for the sake of being nice. This comes as something of a surprise to many people in the wellness, well-being and EQ industry who see niceness as an end in itself. Organisations are not created to deliver niceness. Organisations are created to deliver results, which in the case of private sector companies normally comes in the form of profits. EQ is not an end in itself. It is a means to an end.

EQ is about knowing how to get other people to do things: this places it at the heart of management. EQ is not the same as command and control. It is about being able to use influence to get other people to do things willingly, regardless of whether you have formal control over them or not. To make things happen in most flat, matrix organisations it is not possible to tell people to do things: you have no control over them. You have to find ways of working with them that gain their active support and commitment. A manager who can do this wields power and has effectiveness which goes far beyond the official job title.

EQ is not an innate characteristic which you either have or do not have. There are many people who think they are very good with people. They may even be right. But being liked is not the same thing as being respected and valued in a business context. The effective manager needs to be respected and trusted more than liked. This is not a new insight. In the words of Machiavelli (1469–1527), advising his Prince that *'it is better to be feared than loved, if you cannot be both'*. He then recommends a few exemplary executions to maintain order. Most modern managers prefer to fire people than hang them, if they have to. While such drastic action is not always necessary, the fate of many likeable people is salutary: you often find them languishing in organisational backwaters where their ineffectiveness does not matter.

EQ can be learned. But it cannot be learned as a subject called 'EQ': that takes us straight back to courses which involve hugging trees or abseiling, raft building and parlour games which some people like and many people loathe.

EQ is best learned as a series of discrete skills which have immediate relevance to essential management tasks. The skills-based approach to EQ is distressingly practical for many EQ gurus, which is a good reason to use it here. This chapter will focus on ten EQ-based skills which are at the heart of management in the following sections:

3.1 Motivating people: creating willing followers

3.2 Influencing people: how to sell anything

3.3 Coaching: no more training

3.4 Delegating: doing better by doing less

3.5 Handling conflict: from FEAR to EAR

3.6 Giving informal feedback: making the negative positive

3.7 Managing yourself: personal EQ

3.8 Using time effectively: activity versus achievement

3.9 Surviving the management marathon: from days to decades

3.10 Learning the right behaviours: what managers really want.

The alert reader may wonder if influencing and motivating people are different: they are. Influencing people is often an event. It is about gaining other people's support for an idea or course of action. It is, effectively, a transaction between two people where one person persuades or influences the other person. Motivating people is not about a single transaction: it is about creating a longer-term relationship in which the properly motivated person will do things without having to be told or asked to do it. Well motivated they will go above and beyond expectations and do more than is strictly necessary.

The truly critical reader will have noticed the omission of topics such as change management and political awareness. These topics are covered in detail under PQ, which focuses on how the manager and the organisation interact: EQ focuses more on how the manager and other individuals interact.

Without further ado, let us look at each of these EQ-heavy skills.

3.1 Motivating people: creating willing followers

The basic theories

After a few hundred thousand years of human existence, we may finally be working out what motivates people. To find the answer we will first look at two theories which continue to dominate management thinking. Then we will look at management practice.

For the first theory, imagine any work group that you particularly dislike inside or beyond your organisation. Then imagine a group you particularly enjoy working with. Which of the following two descriptions best fits each group you have chosen?

Description X
They are essentially lazy and work shy. They work mainly for the money, which they will maximise. They will minimise the amount of effort, consistent only with avoiding disciplinary action or loss of earnings. They dislike risk, ambiguity and responsibility. They like leaving all the tough decisions to other people: then they get to complain about the stupid decisions that have been made on their behalf. The best way to control these people is through close monitoring, clear rewards and sanctions, and unambiguous direction.

Description Y
With proper management, these people can be committed: they will work hard and use some degree of creativity to overcome problems without seeking direction; they will seek responsibility rather than avoid it and clearly get more out of work than just a monthly salary. These people can be trusted with delegated tasks, do not need close supervision and will learn and grow in their jobs.

The chances are that you can identify people who belong to both groups. Each group needs to be managed in a different way. In theory, Type X individuals would have characterised the 19th century sweatshop full of unskilled labour and Type Y individuals would characterise the 21st century highly skilled and highly motivated workforce in advanced economies. In practice, both sorts can be found in all kinds of environments. There is also a large element of self-fulfilment here. If you treat people as if they cannot be trusted and need to be controlled, they will start responding to Type X management with Type X behaviour: they will do the minimum to comply with you, but they will demonstrate little commitment. Equally, start managing in Type Y style, and people are likely to respond positively.

These two types of individual were described by MacGregor in *The Human Side of Enterprise* (1960). Roughly 50 years later, the idea of Type X managers (close control, tough managers) and Type Y managers (delegating, trusting types) still exists. The big insights from Type X and Type Y have the virtue of simplicity:

▶ Different people need to be managed in different ways.

▶ Most managers are biased towards either Type X or Type Y.

▶ Therefore managers either need to find the right context where their style works, or they need to be able to adapt their style to different situations. Think of most managers you have worked with: very few are able in practice to switch between Type X and Type Y. Style conflicts are at the heart of most dysfunctional team management problems.

The sophisticated theories

If you want to be sophisticated, you need something a bit more fancy than a straight choice between two alternatives which is as simple as tossing a coin and calling 'X' or 'Y'. So move aside MacGregor and make way for Maslow. Maslow developed the hierarchy of needs in a series of articles and books from 1943 (*A Theory of Human Motivation*) to 1987 (*Motivation and Personality*). It pays to know about Maslow because:

▶ His name and his thinking pervades much management thought: it helps to understand the basis of other people's thinking.

▶ Some of his thinking is genuinely useful.

Maslow's fundamental insight is that we are all needs junkies. There is always something more that we want. Once we have satisfied one level of need, we find there is something more that we want. As children we want a push bike, then we want a motorbike, then a car; to keep up with colleagues we graduate to a sports car, then a private jet to keep up with other CEOs and finally we need our own personal jumbo jet. We laugh at any left on their push bike. Maslow came at this from a psychological background. Economists notice the same effect and call it hedonic adaptation: we adjust up to a higher standard of living more easily than we can adjust down. If you were happy 20 years ago, think if you would still be happy without your iPod, mobile phone, computer, internet connection and cheap flights. Quite how anyone survived 20 years ago is a mystery.

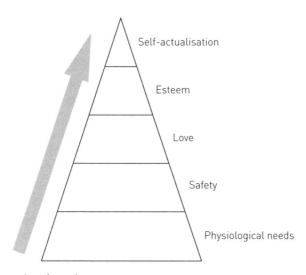

Maslow's hierarchy of needs

At the bottom of Maslow's pyramid (see above) are 'deficiency needs': if we do not have food, water and air (physiological needs) we are likely to be unhappy. Safety is also a deficit need: we are unhappy without shelter and protection. At the top of the pyramid we have 'growth needs'. We want to find meaning and leave a legacy. Much of this echoes the work of other psychologists, and is not greatly controversial. Having said that, Maslow's categories are dangerously close to psychobabble and are largely useless in a management context. Asking the CEO if he is at the love stage is open to misinterpretation. Knowing what stage people are at and knowing what to do about it are not obvious.

Managers need something easier and more practical. So here is a revisionist, unauthorised alternative to Maslow's hierarchy of needs: the management hierarchy of needs.

The management hierarchy of needs

This starts to be easier to work with. Pay and conditions are unlikely to make people happy, but getting them wrong can make people unhappy.

Bonus time!

Working with an investment bank at bonus time was a revelation. One senior trader was given a $300,000 bonus which would be enough for most people. He quickly resigned in disgust (pausing only to deposit the cheque into his account). A close colleague had received $500,000. The problem was that the money was recognising him as less valuable than his colleague. For an executive who was clearly at the recognition and reward stage of his career, this was a terrible blow to his fragile, supersized ego.

At a basic level, a manager can use this framework to see if the basic conditions are in place for having a motivated team:

▶ Do people have a sense of security, or is there constant fear, uncertainty and doubt?

▶ Are the pay and conditions fair and appropriate?

▶ Do team members feel part of a team and a community, or is it survival of the fittest?

▶ Are team members recognised for their contributions, or is all the limelight hogged by one or two?

▶ Is there a worthwhile goal for the team as a whole, and do those goals support the personal aspirations of each individual?

If you can answer these questions positively for your team, you have gone a long way to creating the conditions for a motivated team. But you have not gone all the way: motivation is not about systems on bits of paper. Motivation is an engagement sport: you have to deal with people, not paper, to motivate humans. There will be some managers who turn this hierarchy on its head and rule by fear and the constant threats. People may have to work *for* such bosses to pay the mortgage. Few people choose to work *with* such bosses.

Motivation practice: the magic rule

Maslow only helps us understand how to create the preconditions for a motivated team. He does not tell us how to deal with people on a day-to-day and minute-to-minute basis.

In practice, motivation is happening positively or negatively all the time. Small actions and a few words can raise or lower the motivation thermostat for each individual fast. This means managers have to react fast and well to constantly changing situations: humans are not as predictable as computers.

To find out what made a good manager, we assessed all the managers in our organisation and then asked their teams to assess the managers as well. There was a mountain of data, which was largely indigestible and very confusing. But the more we looked, the more we found that there was one question which accurately predicted how well each manager would be rated by his or her team for intelligence, decision-making ability, charisma, organisational skills, team leadership and all the other qualities we looked for. The question was:

'My boss cares about me and my career' (agree/disagree).

This was so simple and so obvious. People want to be cared for, valued and respected as individuals. Do this, and they will repay your efforts many times over. So the emerging golden rule for motivation is:

Show you care about the future of each individual on your team.

Caring is not about being sugar-sweet nice all the time and one-minute managing people with empty compliments. It takes commitment and hard work on both sides. It involves the following qualities, which will be covered in more detail in later chapters:

▶ Listening: ask open questions and understand the answers before trying to judge people.

▶ Coaching: help people deal with challenges themselves, do not do it for them.

▶ Honesty: deal with uncomfortable truths rather than hide them.

▶ Delivery: always deliver on your half of the psychological contract.

▶ Style: respect the different styles and skills of each team member – work with that rather than force them to fit your style.

▶ Vision and direction: make your department's vision relevant to each individual's personal needs, vision and direction.

If this sounds like hard work, it is. But it is hard work with a purpose: to encourage each team member to contribute to the greatest of his or her ability. And if it all sounds a little complicated, it can be made simple. Even trying to show you care has an immediate impact.

3.2 Influencing people: how to sell anything

Managers need to influence people in the flat world of the matrix organisation: managers lack the power to tell people what to do, so they persuade people to do things. Managers are, effectively, sales people: they sell ideas, priorities, changes and solutions to other departments even if they are not selling products and services to customers.

Influencing is different from motivation. You may influence me to accept your budget recommendation. That is a one-off transaction between you and me. It says nothing about how motivated I might feel working for you, and it says nothing about what motivates me. You have simply secured my agreement for something.

The principles of influencing people

But influencing and motivating share some similar principles. For this, we will return to Maslow and reduce his highly sophisticated hierarchy of needs even further.

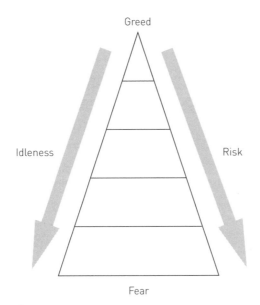

Maslow reduced

Fear, greed, idleness and risk may not be the most uplifting guide to human behaviour, but in management terms it works with unerring accuracy. These are the four dimensions you need to use to influence someone. People want to escape fear, strive for something (greed and hope) but face the two barriers of risk and idleness. A good influencer knows how to play on all four of these dimensions.

Greed

Greed corresponds to Maslow's growth needs: everyone wants something, and when they get it they want something more. To start with, they may want money. But greed is not just about money. People want other things. People like to be recognised. It may be something as simple as praise in public for a job well done. Or it can be the ambitious business person seeking political recognition and public honour through good works and political donations. Effective managers need to find out what the other person wants.

In the daily management practice, greed can be translated into the everyday hopes of colleagues. They have goals and deadlines to meet. They want to look good and to succeed. It does not matter how brilliant your idea may be, if it does not help your colleagues with their agendas you can expect a lukewarm response. Your idea may look great to you: it looks like more work for them.

Fear

Fear is the other side of the coin to greed. It can be a very compelling way of gaining compliance with your idea. In many cases, the proposal is simple: 'If you do not do this the consequences will be. . .' At the first mention of regulatory, legal, health and safety concerns many managers give up: it is not worth taking the risk of letting these things go wrong, even if the risk is very small and the cost is very large. Playing to fear is also used by IT consultants: if you do not implement our very expensive project, then all your mission critical programmes are at risk. Many senior executives lack the technical expertise or will to argue against such fear-based selling.

Fear is also relative. Cost-cutting programmes normally increase fear, not reduce it. That is one reason they are resisted overtly or covertly. To build support for cost-cutting programmes, senior executives play up the even greater fear of what happens if we do not cut costs now. If we do not cut costs now, we might all lose our jobs as the company goes bankrupt: better to lose a few people now than to lose everyone later.

Idleness

There are many things we would like to do. But life is busy. We might want to learn Spanish, get fit, become a painter and get involved in the community. But these things take effort, and in the meantime we have the bills to pay, the dog to feed and the car has broken down again. At work, you have your great idea. But everyone else has other problems to attend to: budgets, meetings, deadlines and crises. Your idea is one more item on an already overcrowded list. Colleagues may like your idea, but not enough to stop working on their priorities to help you achieve yours.

You have to make it easy for people to accept your idea. Show how your idea will make it easier for them to achieve their goals by showing the opposite scenario: opposing your idea will take up huge amounts of their time and will result in lost opportunities. Make it difficult for them to say no.

Risk

Risk is the iceberg that sinks many ideas. It is often unseen and unspoken. Most people are naturally risk averse. Any new idea inevitably carries all sorts of risks with it: it may not work; it may divert resources from other things; it may have unintended consequences; it may lead to a change in the power structure. At any meeting, listen to what happens when any new idea is raised (unless the idea comes from the boss). Immediately people will start asking helpful questions along the lines of 'have you thought of this or that. . .?' These helpful ideas have the effect of:

▶ Showing that the questioner is listening and smart because he or she can identify problems fast.

▶ Killing the idea, because everyone sees how risky it is.

▶ Killing off innovation, because now everyone realises that having an idea is to invite being shot down in public by intellectual questioning.

This is an unproductive outcome which could be avoided if people focused on the benefits and opportunities of an idea, before focusing on all the risks and problems, unhelpfully disguised as helpful questions.

Risk comes in three main flavours:

1   Rational risk: how will this affect the business? People are encouraged to discuss this openly, because business people are meant to be rational.

2   Political risk: how will this idea affect my department? Will it lose or gain resources, priorities and influence as a result of this idea?

3   Emotional risk: how will this idea affect me? Will I have to work harder, be marginalised, have to work with a new boss or develop new skills? People will never raise these risks in public. Instead, they will raise ever more persuasive rational and business objections, which are a cover for their personal and emotional objections.

It pays to know what sort of risk you are dealing with. Many arguments become increasingly bitter over apparently logical issues. When this happens both sides start digging ever deeper holes, using logic to defend political and emotional positions. The best solution is to stop digging. Stop the discussion and find some time in private when the real issues can be raised and dealt with.

As with idleness, it pays to reverse the risk equation. Show, if possible, that the risks of doing nothing significantly outweigh the risks of doing what you propose. Risk avoidance is a powerful way of gaining compliance. Insurance is sold entirely on the idea of risk avoidance. Government cannot persuade us to pay taxes or wear seat belts, but it makes the risks of not doing so high enough so that most people comply.

Know what to sell: products versus solutions

History is littered with brilliant ideas which failed. Clive Sinclair, a British inventor, developed a vehicle called the C5: it was all electric and would revolutionise urban transport. It might have done, if people had been able to stop laughing at the bug-like vehicle which was so low to the ground that it needed a flag at its rear to alert other road users to its existence. It disappeared faster than its backer's funding into a black hole.

It is not just boffins who get carried away with their own ideas. We have all had to sit through presentations where someone drones on about some new miracle management theory they have discovered.

The boffins and the presenters fall into the same trap: they are focused on their own ideas, not on other people's needs. They are like irritating versions of the double-glazing sales people who can only sell you what they have, not what you want.

Do not bore people with your great product or idea. You may get lucky, and they may share your interest. But luck is not a method. To increase your odds of success you need to set aside your ideas and imagine what the world looks like from their perspective. Understand what their hopes and fears are and tap into them. Show how you can provide a solution to their problem. If your product or idea is part of a solution to their problem, you will engage their interest.

Effective influencing does not start with your idea. It starts with what the other person wants.

The process of influencing people

This is a process which I have used to sell nappies in Birmingham, to sell the idea of starting a new bank and to get countless recommendations accepted in different organisations and countries. The process combines a logical and emotional flow designed to make it easy for the other person to agree, and difficult for them to disagree. The flow is not original: it is based on the sales disciplines that Procter & Gamble instils in its sales force.

The process follows the influencing principles of fear, greed, idleness and risk but adds a special start and a special finish.

1 The start: preparation and the social introduction

There is a logical and emotional element to the start. The logical element is called preparation. Preparation is about asking some basic questions:

- What are the benefits of my idea to the other person?
- What are the risks from their perspective?
- How can I make it easy for them to agree?
- What is their style of working, and how can I get along with them best?
- What is the best time to approach them?

▶ Have I got all the material I need to support my discussion with them?

These are very obvious questions. They are very rarely asked, and you can look surprisingly smart by asking them when a team member comes and asks your advice on how to plan an influencing meeting.

The emotional element of the start is social. This does not mean passing the time of day talking about the weather. The social start to a meeting serves to set the meeting up for success. A good start to the meeting will ensure:

▶ You are meeting at a convenient time.

▶ You have anchored the meeting around the core topic.

▶ You have built some trust and rapport with the other person.

This social start needs only a few questions and statements such as:

▶ 'Thank you for meeting me. Is this still a convenient time?'

▶ 'You look as busy as ever' (inviting them to download their problems for a moment to an empathetic ear: if they are too busy, you will find out now).

▶ 'As promised, I have to ask your advice about. . .' You have now anchored the conversation, and you have not put yourself into selling mode: you are asking for advice and help.

Everyone has their own way of going through the social start: the important thing is to make sure that the other person is ready to talk about your subject. If they are not, find another time. If you are meeting a person for the first time, there is more socialising you will need to do. Typically, such socialising is around finding a common interest, common acquaintances or common professional background. The purpose of such social chat is to build a basic level of trust by finding common experiences, values and outlooks.

2 Agree the problem: what is the fear we are dealing with?

Here, you have to able to answer one question going through the mind of the person you are dealing with:

'Why should I be worried about this problem now?'

They have plenty of other things to worry about, without you adding to their to-do list.

You need to identify not just the problem, but who owns the problem. If you are helping the other person with one of their challenges, you are more likely to find an open door and an available diary than if you are solving your own problem. A common intermediate step is to be addressing a challenge which has come down from on high: from a boss who both of you share. The purpose of agreeing the problem is to force attention and gain legitimacy for the issue, which can be:

▶ Rational: there is a big challenge for the whole organisation and we have the numbers to show it.

▶ Emotional: I can help you with your agenda and challenges.

▶ Political: we have to sort this out for our common boss.

To make the problem compelling, you have to show it is important, urgent and that the other person has a role to play in sorting it out.

Do not even start to suggest a solution until there is hard agreement about the nature of the challenge. Invite them to talk about it: hear and understand their perspective. As you listen you can work out how to pitch your idea so that it hits all the right buttons and avoids the red flags, which might stop the idea from their perspective.

3 Outline the benefits of resolving the problem

In business, the most compelling business case is financial. It is very hard to argue against a credible and compelling business case: '$1,000 invested now will save $2,000 tomorrow'. The critical issue is whether anyone believes the claim. The claim must be credible: this can be achieved through a combination of rigorous analysis and, more importantly, validation by trusted third parties: finance validates the financial numbers, marketing validates the customer and market assumptions, and operations and IT validate their parts of the equation.

Not all benefits are financial. Non-financial business cases can be both quantifiable ('we will recruit more top graduates next year') and qualitative ('this is important for morale').

At this point, there should still be no mention of your idea or solution. Once the other person has agreed to both the problem and the benefits of solving the solution, then the only discussion is 'How do we best get there?' Then they are ready to hear your idea: even if they do not like it, they are now in a position where they are not just trying to evaluate your idea, but they are helping you find a path from the problem to the solution.

4 Explain how it works: make it easy for them

Provide a simple explanation of your idea. Keep it short. Show that you do not need them to do everything: you need a limited amount of support in one critical area to progress. Then quickly move on to the next stage.

5 Pre-empt any objections: remove the risk

If you have done your preparation well, and you have listened to them when you were discussing the original problem, this should be easy: you should know exactly what their concerns should be. Do not hide from these objections: use them as a chance to shine. If you now say: 'I think there are three real concerns with this approach. . .' and these concerns reflect the major concerns of the other person, you will suddenly have them on your side. They are no longer going to have to challenge you with their objections: you are inviting them to work with you on solving the concerns. The nature of the discussion has changed completely.

If the objections start to flow at this point, do not engage in fighting each objection in an ever bloodier version of corporate trench warfare. Go back to stage 2: check that you both agree on the problem, then agree on the benefits of solving the problem. You need to create a problem-solving atmosphere, not a problem-generating atmosphere.

6 Close

Most people are not psychic: they will not know exactly what you want. You have to ask them for it. They expect you to ask: otherwise it has been a pretty pointless meeting. But this is where many executives fail. They are too self-effacing to ask for the next steps. But there are four simple ways of asking for the next steps, which make it quite difficult for the other person to refuse:

1   The direct close: 'Can we buy the special widgets?'

2   The alternative close: 'Should we buy the widgets in one big order or split the order?'

3   The assumed close: 'So we are agreed that we are buying 100,000 yellow widgets.'

4   The action close: 'I will raise the widgets order and send it over to you.'

The weakest close is the direct one, because you invite people to say 'no'. The sneakiest, and often most effective, is the alternative close. You are not giving them the option of saying no to the widget order: you are only inviting them to choose how they should be ordered. The assumed close is a power close, because it takes quite a strong person to speak up, especially in a public meeting, and disagree.

Summary of the process

1   The start: preparation and the social introduction

2   Agree the problem: what is the fear we are dealing with?

3   Outline the benefits of resolving the problem

4   Explain how it works: make it easy for them

5   Pre-empt any objections: remove the risk

6   Close

Creating the partnership: how to ask for a billion dollars

I decided to start a bank. There was one small problem: I needed about a billion dollars to start it. As an unemployed individual on the street, I found that banks were not queuing at my door to cough up the dough.

So I followed the influencing model over the next few months.

1 The start

Plenty of detailed preparation went into building the business case and getting it validated by senior bankers who had credibility in the industry. Through them I secured meetings with various CEOs and chairmen of different banks. I focused mainly on one bank which had a hole in its portfolio which this idea filled.

➤

---

2 Agree the problem

The bank quickly agreed that there was a challenge and an opportunity in the area I had identified.

3 Outline the benefits

The business case was compelling financially. What was more important was that it had been validated by respected figures in the industry. At this point, the CEO leaned over the coffee table and asked:

> 'How much will it take to start this?'
>
> 'About a billion over five years, mostly success capital,' I said with a well-rehearsed answer, making sure I said billion, not million.
>
> 'Dollars or pounds?' he asked
>
> 'Pounds,' I said quickly, deciding to give myself another few hundred million dollars of room to manoeuvre.

At this point, I had avoided giving him any detailed data. There was no PowerPoint presentation. All the discussions had been set up as partnership discussions: I was not going in to plead my case or be a sales person. I was there to help craft an opportunity with him. If I had offered any numbers, they would have been massacred by his accountants who would show that it did not comply with their arcane ways of measuring and allocating banking capital. Instead, we agreed that he would offer up a couple of employees to help me craft the required paper for the board.

4 Explain how it works and 5 Pre-empt any objections

By this stage I was not selling. I was working in partnership with the CEO to find a way forward. Selling is difficult: working together to solve a problem is easy. This is the position that a successful sales person needs to reach. So designing the detailed solution happened in partnership with the CEO's team, rather than me having to double guess all their arcane requirements.

6 Close

They now moved one step ahead of me: they bought another bank and decided to implement the idea themselves. There is no legal protection for a business idea. We live and learn. . .

Influencing: two secret rules

1 The listening rule

All great influencers and sales people share a common characteristic: they have two ears and one mouth. If you have this, then you are halfway to becoming a very good influencer. Good influencers not only have two ears and one mouth: they use them in that proportion. Influencing is not about selling and telling. It is about listening well. If you listen twice as much as you talk, you are well on the way to success.

2 The partnership rule

Bosses and clients are used to acting as judges: they judge all the ideas coming before them. This is not a constructive relationship. It typically involves the plaintiff pitching his case with a stack of PowerPoint slides and memos to impress the judge. The judge then picks a few holes in the presentation to show she is smart and decides for or against the plaintiff.

A much better way is to turn the boss or client into a partner and a coach. Show that you are there to help with their problem or opportunity, not just to advance your own agenda. Throw away the PowerPoint slides. Power-Point slides are the badge of shame that junior staff and sales people have to wear. Colleagues do not talk to each other over a stack of slides: they talk to each other over a cup of coffee. By throwing away the slides you:

▶ avoid getting locked into the logic flow of the slides

▶ can react flexibly to what colleagues are saying

▶ create the opportunity to listen and discuss, like colleagues, rather than present like a plaintiff

▶ are forced to prepare very closely around the logical and emotional flow of the discussion you want to have

▶ avoid getting trapped into arguments about detail and data.

Do not worry about the data. Have a few killer facts in your mind. Then you can offer to send across the detail later.

3.3 Coaching: no more training

In most sports there are players and there are coaches. Players play and coaches coach, but rarely do coaches play or players coach. There is a huge divide between the two. The best players rarely make the best coaches. The best coaches were often journeymen players.

In management, things are not quite so clear-cut, with unfortunate consequences. The good player (IT specialist, sales person or trader) gets promoted and their natural instinct is to go on playing. Playing is what got them promoted and there seems little point in changing a winning formula. But formulas only win if conditions remain the same. Promotion changes everything.

The newly promoted player naturally wants to take on all the most challenging tasks. This is precisely the wrong approach. The role of the coach is not to make all the tackles and score all the goals for the team. The role of the coach is to help the team achieve all these things, to bring out the best in each individual and to organise members effectively. The more the coach tries to be the best player, the more the team learns dependency. They rely on the coach to do everything. The coach thinks this shows the team is weak, so redoubles already Herculean efforts to make up for the team's weaknesses. The coach is playing ever harder to achieve ever worse results with a team that becomes ever more dependent. Eventually, there is an explosion and the coach is fired or gives up in total exhaustion.

The hardest lesson to learn for the newly promoted manager is to move from playing to coaching. Coaching is important because it:

▶ helps each individual grow their talents

▶ lightens the load of the team leader and other team members

▶ enables the team leader to focus on the right activities, rather than fire fighting.

Coaching, like influencing, is about listening and asking smart questions. This is easier to say than to do. When a team member comes to you looking for advice, the overwhelming instinct is to give them the answer. As soon as you do that, you have become a player again and the team member has learned nothing except to depend on you even more. Giving the answer may be quick in the short term, but creates a dependent team long term that will suck out all your time and energy. If you help members discover the answer for themselves you may also find that they have a better answer than the one you first thought of. At minimum, they will feel more commitment to a solution they have created than you have imposed on them.

There are many coaching models available. In essence, they all boil down to roughly the same four-step process. For alliterative purposes, we will arrange them into the four Os:

1 objectives

2 overview

3 options

4 outcome.

At each stage, it is more important to know the right questions than to have the right answers. The coach brings a different perspective. This is fundamentally different from the idea of training, in which the trainer instructs people on exactly how to do something. The coach does not tell someone what to do. The coach helps each person discover what works for them. Trainers tell, coaches ask. Trainers have a set method which they enforce. Coaches can see things from different angles. Most managers default to the safety of training: 'do it my way'. This is safe in the short term, but it fails to help each team member achieve their full potential.

1 Objectives

Step one is to understand the problem we are solving: this is the same logic as the influencing model outlined above:

> What is it that you want to focus on, achieve, review today?

2 Overview

Next steps are to gather all the facts, before forming a view or making a judgement. This takes some gentle probing, in which you encourage discussion of different perspectives. Do not get locked into the world view of the person being coached: you have to help them see a broader perspective.

Why is this important to you?

What is the current situation?

How do other people see this?

How do you know they see it that way?

What are the potential consequences, good or bad, of this?

3 Options

This is where you get them to take responsibility and control. Do not give them the answer, even if you think you have it. Let them discover the answer which will work for them. Push them to think of more than one option. In very difficult situations there may not be much they can control: urge them to find something they can control. The more people feel a sense of control over their destiny, the less anxious they will feel. Then get them to evaluate the options they have generated.

What choices do you have?

What can you control or influence?

Have you seen anyone face anything like this before? What did they do?

How would you evaluate the benefits, risks and consequences of each option?

4 Outcomes

Finally, drive to action. Make sure that they have thought through the barriers and obstacles to success and that they know the next steps.

What happens next?

What will prevent you doing this?

How can I help you?

By now, you will have noticed some familiar themes running through both influencing and coaching:

- ▶ listening is more important than talking
- ▶ questions are at least as important as answers
- ▶ understand the question before offering the answer.

These may seem very obvious lessons. The reason for spelling them out is that very few managers consistently follow these principles. By following them, you will start to stand out from the crowd.

3.4 Delegating: doing better by doing less

Many managers find it difficult to delegate. Common excuses include:

▶ This is too important to delegate.

▶ This is too urgent: I need to do it myself.

▶ The team is not strong enough yet, they are not ready.

▶ Only I have the skills to do this.

▶ The team already has too much to do.

▶ I cannot risk letting the team screw up on this one.

All these excuses come down to lack of trust in the team and an inflated sense of the manager's unique skill. And they all condemn the manager to becoming overworked and the team to becoming overdependent on the manager. The team will only grow if the manager can delegate and trust it.

Delegating and coaching go hand in hand. They both ensure that managers achieve the core task of management: getting other people to do things. The process of delegation is simple:

1 Work out what you can delegate

In practice, there is very little you cannot delegate: evaluations, promotions, disciplinary procedure, resource allocation, team formation are all the preserve of the manager. Assume that everything else should be delegated. Many managers work on the opposite assumption: they delegate as an exception, not as a rule. You should find that you delegate a mixture of fairly routine administrative and maintenance activities, combined with a few more stretching and engaging initiatives.

2 Know your team

Think carefully about who is best for which tasks. Balance their current capabilities versus their ability to learn and grow by doing the task. If a person is 80 per cent ready, then trust them. This can be nerve-wracking as you see them struggle with stuff which would be easy for you, but that is the best way they will learn. Once they have learned, they become more productive and valuable members of your team. Balance out the workload across the team.

3 Set clear objectives

When briefing a team member you need to give clarity and certainty to four things:

1   the expected outcome

2   when the outcome must be achieved

3   the reasons behind the goals you have set

4   intermediate objectives which let both of you know if things are on track.

If your team understands why you are making a request, they will be in a much better position to respond to questions and challenges as they arise, instead of having to refer back to you.

4 Discuss the process

You can be clear about the goals, but need to be flexible over the means. This becomes a negotiation around several key topics:

▶ How much resource (people, skills, budget) will be available to the team?

▶ How much decision-making authority will it have?

▶ How often will it be necessary to report?

▶ What is the best approach to take?

▶ Who else needs to be involved?

▶ How can the manager help in removing roadblocks, dealing with the politics?

This may be more than one conversation. The objective of this step is partly to set the team up for success. Equally, discussion gives the team a sense of ownership over the process. It might even come up with a really smart way of tackling the task which you had not thought about before.

5 Follow up

You are delegating, not abdicating, responsibility. You are still responsible for the final outcome. Three key elements of the follow-up are:

1   Be available to coach as required.
2   Check up on progress formally and informally as discussed with the team at the start of the task.
3   Recognise its contribution and success when it has completed the task.

Some managers try to steal the limelight at the end of a successful effort by their team. This demoralises the team and does not help the manager. The manager looks much better to his bosses if he can show that he can build and manage a great team, than if he pretends to do all the hard work as a one-man band.

How not to delegate

David was a manager from hell. He genuinely believed he was good at delegating because he delegated a lot. What this meant in practice was that he delegated all the rubbish. This would be a toxic mix of the routine stuff that anyone could do, plus a few projects which were known as 'hospital passes'. They were so late or so badly messed up that the person receiving the project was more or less certain to land up in career hospital. The manager was effectively delegating all the blame. He was very good at this.

To really mess his team up he would give vague instructions about what he wanted and then shout at people when they failed to read his mind properly and provide exactly what he wanted. His vagueness also allowed him to change his mind frequently, which led to endless late nights and frustration as the team reworked projects for him.

➤

> Because he never really trusted his teams, he would ask for constant updates. More time was spent updating him than doing the work. The lack of trust was corrosive of team spirit and used up all the team's time.
>
> If, by some chance, a good result emerged from this method, David was very keen to make sure that everyone knew he was responsible for the outcomes. Setbacks were invariably the fault of his inadequate team. Eventually, this became a self-fulfilling statement. Anyone who was any good found another boss, another department or another company to work for. He was left with the weakest players, which reinforced his belief that he could trust no one with delegated work. The misery cycle was complete, and was only broken when David finally left the company.

3.5 Handling conflict: from FEAR to EAR

Conflict is the natural state for most organisations. The most intense conflict is not against rival organisations. Conflicts are largely invisible on a day-to-day basis for most managers: HR, IT and operations staff are too focused on dealing with their immediate functional challenges to worry about marketplace competition. The real competition is not external: it is internal. The biggest threat to most managers is not a rival organisation: it is a rival manager who may be sitting at a desk near you.

In a well-run organisation, this conflict is healthy. Conflict is the way that the battle for resources and priorities in the organisation are decided. There is a limited pool of management time, money, resource and skills. There is a limited pot of potential promotions, bonuses and pay rises. Every department, function and business unit will have a different perspective on how that limited pot should be divided up. The inevitable consequence is rivalry and conflict between managers within an organisation.

This conflict can be productive. It forces managers to show that they have the best way of using the limited resources of the organisation. Occasionally, this competitive conflict becomes dysfunctional. Dysfunctional conflict comes in two flavours:

- cold wars
- hot wars.

Cold wars are basically political and are an essential reality of management. Hot wars tend to be emotional, flaring up in an instant. Neither side is likely to come out looking good. But there is a question of survival: handle it badly and you can become damaged goods in the organisation.

Starting a hot war

We were standing in the school corridor, surrounded by well-behaved children. It was a school in a tough area achieving great results. My colleague dismissed it as old-fashioned. This was, perhaps, not the ideal moment to inform him that he was being arrogant and narrow-minded.

The reaction was spectacular. His eyes bulged. His face went crimson and the veins on his neck popped out. Spittle spewed from his mouth as he shouted, 'I have never been so insulted in all his life.' He quickly got a good audience for his performance.

At this stage I wanted to reply, 'In that case, no one has been trying.' It would have been fun to watch his reaction, and I really did not care what he thought any more. He was now in full raging and ranting mode. I needed to decide fast what to do next. . .

Principle one: know which battles to fight

Sun-Tsu, the Chinese philosopher, wrote *The Art of War* about 2,350 years ago. Perhaps his most useful insight was in knowing when to fight. He gave three rules for fighting:

1 *Only fight if the prize is worth fighting for.* Most corporate battles are over small things: save your ammunition and personal credibility for the big battles. On small things, it is often easier to do a trade: concede one point and gain another in return.

2 *Only fight if you know you are going to win.* On Wall Street, the saying goes: 'If you don't know who the fall guy is, you are.' The last thing you want is a good clean fight: you want a completely unfair fight where you are sure to win. This is not just about having the best arguments. It is about having all your allies lined up well in advance.

3   *Only fight if there is no other way of achieving your goal.* Enemies are not good for your career. Find a way of co-opting people onto your agenda; align your goals with theirs; get an intermediary to broker a deal; do a trade with them over interests, timing, priorities or resources. To turn Clausewitz (a military philosopher) on his head: 'diplomacy is a continuation of war by other means'. Diplomacy is the bloodless way of achieving your goals.

All three of these conditions need to be in place to make it worth fighting. But when you do fight, fight hard. Remember the words of Colonel Tim Collins to his troops as he sent them into war during the second Iraq conflict: 'If you are ferocious in battle remember to be magnanimous in victory.' You will need to win the peace as well as winning the war.

Deciding whether to fight

As my colleague's arms and arguments got carried away, I had a chance to think through the rules of war:

1   *Is there a prize worth fighting for?* None, other than my own dignity: the looks from the children showed that neither my colleague nor I had much dignity left anyway.

2   *Am I sure to win?* Since I did not know what I was fighting for, this seemed unlikely. There was no clear winning strategy.

3   *Is there another way of achieving my goal?* Perhaps the goal had already been achieved: his complacency and cynicism had been challenged.

Fighting looked pointless. The only question was: what to do next? I was feeling offended by his insults to me. I did not want to argue back. I wanted to hit him. He was still ranting, I had a moment or two to gather myself. . .

Principle two: from FEAR to EAR

Human instinct trumps human reason, especially at moments of stress and conflict. The natural reaction to danger is the flight or fight reaction, spurred on by a good deal of fear. In the context of your organisation, these are deeply unhelpful instincts. Running away or fighting the CEO at the first hint of a challenge could become a career limiting move. We have to find a way of managing our feelings.

The FEAR instinct can be summarised as:

- **F**ight furiously
- **E**ngage enemy emotionally
- **A**rgue against all-comers
- **R**etaliate, refute reason.

Like flight and fight, the FEAR reaction is not helpful. It is, however, a potentially memorable way to spend your last day with an employer. The first step in overcoming the FEAR reaction is to recognise it. Once we recognise it, we can start to control it. In training sessions, we ask managers how they deal with the FEAR reaction. Some of the more original ways of managing personal stress include:

- Become a fly on the wall: watch yourself and decide on the best course of action from this out-of-body position.
- Imagine what the person you most admire would do in this situation, and try it.
- Imagine the other person as a baby throwing its toys out of the pram: it is hard to get angry with a baby in a tantrum.
- Imagine the other person wearing a tutu: becoming angry with a fat 50-year-old in a tutu is very difficult.
- Quietly pull out your imaginary Kalashnikov and mow them down as you smile at them. As they do not know you are shooting them, they cannot even retaliate.
- Focus on breathing: breathe deeply and slowly, regain control of your body and emotions.
- Count to ten before replying. Give yourself time to think, avoid inflaming the discussion any more and let the other person's storm blow itself out.
- Go to your happy place: everyone has a place in their heads which is safe and secure. Go there, take stock and then proceed.

All these tricks help achieve the essential first three goals:

1 Regain personal control.
2 Buy time to think.

3   Let the storm blow itself out.

It is extraordinarily difficult to sustain anger for more than two minutes, although those two minutes can feel like an eternity. The only way to sustain the anger is to give it some more fuel. Give the angry person no fuel, and they will run out of steam fast. Fuel comes in several forms:

▶ Engaging with them emotionally.

▶ Justifying and defending your position, which will lead to them arguing even more intensely about why you are wrong.

▶ Using body language to show how angry, upset or dismissive you feel.

Stopping the war

There was nothing worth fighting for. The best thing to do was to get the frothing, foaming fury to calm down. So I threw away the last of my pride and dignity and did the hardest thing of all: I apologised.

He then threw the apology back in my face. I was insulted. Perhaps I should have hit him after all. But I stayed in control and apologised again. He threw the apology back in my face again. He could not hear reason. He was so self-consumed in his anger he could not see beyond the red mist. I had to stay patient and ignore the invitations to justify myself and provoke more warfare. I was finding it very hard to stay restrained. After five attempts, he finally calmed down.

Now to win the peace. . .

It is better to win a friend than win an argument. Winning a friend is the best way to win the argument. A friend is more likely to listen to reason and compromise than an enemy. A simple way of doing this is to remove the F from FEAR. What remains is EAR, which is what you should be using. Listening is a far better way of gaining agreement than talking and persuading. EAR stands for:

▶ Empathise.

▶ Agree the problem.

▶ Resolve the way forward.

Empathise

Some people appear naturally empathetic. The rest of us have to learn the skill. Fortunately, it is quite easy. You do not have to become a fully qualified shrink, a neuro-linguistic programming expert or an agony aunt to become empathetic. Here are three simple ways in which you can become more empathetic in your dealings with colleagues:

1 *Stop talking at them.* Instead, let them hear the voice of perfect reason and harmony: their own voice. Do not feel the need to fill a silence. Let them fill the silence with their own wisdom. Silence is a wonderful way of letting opponents talk themselves into submission, buyers talk themselves into agreement and lovers talk themselves into bed.

2 *Listen actively.* Show that you are listening by paraphrasing back what you heard them say. Do not repeat what they said: this appears artificial. Show that you have absorbed what they said and have interpreted it. If you misinterpreted, they will quickly tell you and you avoid misunderstanding. If you interpreted correctly, they will think that you are wonderful for hearing their wisdom so well.

3 *Ask open questions.* Open questions encourage people to talk more. A closed question encourages a yes/no answer which kills the conversation and has the potential to create conflict if the answer is 'no'. Open questions often start with a 'what', 'how' or 'why'. These are difficult to answer with a 'yes' or 'no'.

Agree the problem

Many conflicts are about different agendas and priorities. Finance is focused on cost control and marketing is focused on revenue generation. The result can be a dialogue of the deaf. If the problem remains decreasing costs versus raising revenues, there is no rational discussion to be had. So the two sides need to agree a common way of looking at the challenge. In reality, both marketing and finance should want to increase profitability of the organisation. Once both sides agree a common challenge, they can agree a common way forward: marketing investment needs to show an adequate return to shareholders. There is still plenty of discussion and debate, but at least both sides are now working towards the same goal and share the same language.

This is a stunningly obvious point, which is why it is normally missed. There is a real art form in changing the nature of the conflict from a win/lose to a win/win. Costs versus revenues is a win/lose argument. Increasing profitability can become a win/win for both sides.

Resolve the way forward

This rational discussion can only happen when both sides have got past the emotional problems of the hot war and when they have agreed the common problem. In practice, this is often the easiest part of the discussion. If you are jointly trying to find a way through you are likely to succeed. If you are trying to fight your way past each other in opposite directions, you will find it difficult to make progress.

This is, hopefully, a rational discussion based on emotionally and politically stable foundations. Because it is a rational discussion, it is covered in detail under section 2.4: Solving problems.

By now you may have noticed that IQ, EQ and PQ have reared their ugly heads again. The EAR process of resolving a hot conflict pulls together the three core management skills:

▶ EQ: empathise, remove the emotional heat of the moment

▶ PQ: agree the common problem, align agendas

▶ IQ: solve the problem and agree the way forward

Winning the peace

After we had both calmed down, we realised we had both acted unwisely. Shame-faced we made peace. As we did so, we quickly realised we both shared the same ambition of helping achieve greatness in the most challenging urban schools. We realised we both saw many of the same opportunities and we disagreed only on detail. We could now make progress and win together: he is the best of allies anyone could ask for in such a tough task.

Of course, the real lesson has nothing to do with dealing with conflict. The real lesson is that it is much smarter to avoid creating the conflict in the first place. The art of giving feedback constructively is dealt with in the next

---

section. Giving the wrong person the wrong feedback at the wrong time and in the wrong place was not smart.

3.6 Giving informal feedback: making the negative positive

Managing would be much easier if it did not involve people. At the heart of management is the idea of making things happen through other people. We need to get the best out of our team and our colleagues. This requires a fine balance of providing support and encouragement (positive feedback) and improving performance (constructive feedback). If that is the theory, the reality for many team members and managers is a combination of no feedback (instead of positive feedback) and negative feedback (instead of constructive feedback).

If nothing else, it is worth keeping in mind the perceived reality and the ideal to which we might aspire:

Perceived reality	Ideal feedback
No feedback	Positive feedback
Negative feedback	Constructive feedback

Principle one: give positive feedback

Positive feedback is not simply about being nice to people. Positive feedback helps because it:

- ▶ encourages the right sort of behaviour
- ▶ builds the confidence of the recipient of the feedback
- ▶ opens up a non-threatening dialogue about performance, making coaching easier
- ▶ raises both individual and team morale.

Power of positive feedback

John Timpson owns a chain of shoe repair shops which bear his name. He sets himself the goal of giving ten pieces of positive feedback for each piece of negative feedback. This has a powerful effect. It highlights and reinforces the sort of behaviour and values he wants to encourage. Praise sets the norm and quietly discourages inappropriate behaviour. By praising a shop worker who returns some money a customer has lost, he sets the standard: staff know that this is a company which encourages honesty and fair dealing. It is a more powerful way of communicating the message than putting in rule books, procedures and sanctions designed to punish the wrong sorts of behaviour. Praise builds a culture of commitment: rules build a culture of compliance.

There are good and bad ways of giving even positive feedback. Essentially, the principles are the same as when giving effective constructive feedback, outlined below.

Principle two: make constructive feedback constructive

Constructive feedback is the art of changing perspectives and behaviours. There are some tried and tested ways of doing this well and poorly. The four basic steps of giving constructive feedback are:

1   Find the right time and the right place.
2   Be specific, not general and focus on behaviour not the person.
3   Pause.
4   Solve the problem and move to next steps.

1 Find the right time and the right place

Constructive feedback requires a change in perspective or behaviour: that implies criticism of current behaviour. People do not like criticism, especially in public:

▶   Give the feedback in private, not in public. Do not force someone to defend themselves in public or shame them in public: it will get a negative reaction.

▶ Give the feedback near enough to the actual event for it to be fresh in the memory, but not if the person is still upset or angry about what has just happened. Let them calm down first: reassure them that you are not going to bite their head off. Then they may start to transition from an emotional state to a more rational state.

The clear difference with positive feedback is that positive feedback is often best in public, as well as in private. People like public recognition, and it sends a signal to the rest of the team about the sorts of behaviours which you believe are important to the success of the team.

2 Be specific, not general and focus on behaviour not the person

Telling someone that they are unprofessional is, in itself, unprofessional. It is very general and it is an attack on the person. It invites a fight rather than a change in behaviour. Take the concern and ask yourself why you made that judgement. Then focus on the specific behaviours that led to that comment. For instance, 'I noticed you have turned up late to work four days in a row,' is a factual description of behaviour. If they agree with this, you may be ready for the next step.

The same principle applies with positive feedback. Saying, 'I think you are a wonderful person,' is unhelpful: it is not actionable and probably sounds insincere. Saying, 'That solution you came up with on customer service was very creative, and it has worked,' is specific.

Choice of language is important here. Generalisations such as 'never', 'always' and 'everyone' are unlikely to be accurate and will inflame things.

3 Pause

Give the other person a chance to react. There are several ways of doing this:

▶ Shut up. There is no need to fill the air with your opinions. Give them space to respond.

▶ Ask an open question or invite a response: 'Lateness is not like you. I don't understand why it is suddenly happening.'

▶ Reflect on how it affects you personally: 'It has made life difficult for me because. . .' Only use reflection as a prompt if the first two options are not generating a response.

At this point you may find they have a domestic crisis, or they have been working exceedingly late or there may be some other reason which you can work on together. You are inviting the other person to become a partner in solving a joint problem, rather than being a boss that is going to scold a team member like a parent scolding a child. You are trying to construct an adult-to-adult conversation, not a parent-child script.

Do not move to the next stage unless you can:

▶ Agree the problem, or at least the symptoms of a problem (lateness).

▶ Agree that the problem needs to be solved: it is important and relevant.

▶ Agree the causes of the problem.

If you do not have these agreements in place, you may find the discussion going round in circles, from symptoms to causes to facts to solutions and who is to blame.

In this pause, let the other person reflect on why things are happening the way they are. Simply saying 'I never expect to see you late again' is unhelpful. You may be addressing the symptom of a problem (lateness) not its cause (domestic crises, late-night working, disenchantment with work). Trying to remove the spots from a child's face with spot remover is not going to work if the child has measles: to cure the symptoms you have to cure the cause of the problem.

4 Solve the problem and move to the next steps

The trick here is to make it their solution: you want them to feel a sense of commitment to an idea which they own. If you have done the groundwork properly, you will now be able to go into coaching mode, rather than feedback mode. Follow the principles outlined in coaching in section 3.3.

Questions, not answers, lie at the heart of good coaching. Let the other person discover the answer for themselves. If they discover the answer:

▶ They will be more committed to their answer than an answer you impose on them.

▶ There is a risk that their answer may be better than the one you originally had in mind. It is a risk worth taking.

Constructive feedback: questions versus answers

I was ready for an ear bashing from the partner. I had not really delivered on a project. I knew and he knew, even if the client did not really know it. I went to his office and closed the door with my heart in my boots. It felt like going to see the head teacher on a detention. I was not looking forward to the interview.

He then surprised me. He said 'You are definitely one of our high-potential associates. Maybe one of the best.' He then went on to describe the specific events that led him to that conclusion. Then, with just a hint of a wry smile, he asked, 'How did you feel about the last project?'

With very little coaxing I spilled the beans on how bad it was and why it was so bad. So he asked me how I would handle things in future. I knew what I wanted to do. We discussed various ideas and agreed a plan. He asked if I needed any help and we agreed to meet again in a couple of weeks to see how things were going.

I had gone into the room feeling bad, but I left feeling good. I knew what I had to do. I had a supportive boss.

After I left, I realised that he had never made any criticism and never offered any solution. He had just asked a few questions. I had done all the work for him. As I result, I owned the problem and the solution. I left the room committed to action, rather than feeling resentful about a ticking off.

3.7 Managing yourself: personal EQ

It is hard to manage other people if you cannot manage yourself. From a professional perspective, personal EQ covers three major topics:

1   self-motivation

2   self-awareness

3   self-adjustment.

In your personal life, EQ covers much more ground and gets into the whole wellness arena. For those who are interested, there are great resources out there to help. Check out the works by Seligman and Baylis who are the leaders in the wellness movement in the USA and UK respectively.

1 Self-motivation

EQ skills are often talked about as traits which you either have or you do not have. This is profoundly unhelpful: fail some half-witted pseudo-psychological test and you can be condemned to being an also ran.

In EQ terms, successful managers are typically expected to have the following traits:

▶ initiative

▶ drive

▶ optimism

▶ commitment

▶ persistence.

As you look at the list, the normal human reaction is to think we all have all those traits. In good times we probably do. In good times we are probably able to perform well as a result. The question is whether we show the same traits under stress over weeks, months and years. Everyone has a point at which their initiative, drive, optimism, commitment and persistence start to flag. In all careers there can be several years in a row which seem like an exercise in pushing water uphill.

Instead of administering a simplistic personality test to see if you have the self-motivation to succeed, look instead at your context. If you show the right traits, you are probably in the right context. If you are finding it difficult to show the right stuff, you may well have the wrong context in terms of assignment, boss, organisation, location or career. You can only excel at what you enjoy, so you have to find the context in which you will be able to find self-motivation to perform well.

Self-motivation is clearly something to do with you. The reality behind the hype of all the personal makeover consultants is that most people do not change dramatically. But people can change their context dramatically, with equally dramatic impact on their self-motivation and performance.

Self-motivation is about finding the right context as much as it is about finding the right self.

2 Self-awareness

Self-awareness is more dangerous EQ territory. It can quickly plunge into navel gazing about your personality, childhood and meaning in life. These are important things to deal with as a human being. From a management perspective, self-awareness is not about navel gazing. Brutally, managers do not care what sort of childhood the accountant had, as long as the month-end accounts are closed accurately and on time.

For managers the heart of self-awareness starts by understanding how you affect other people. This is a key point worth emphasising:

Self awareness starts by understanding how you affect other people.

Most of this chapter has focused on how you can affect, influence and motivate other people by seeing the world through their eyes. In addition to this, you need to be able to read how they are reacting to you. Probably the least useful form of feedback is the annual evaluation from the boss: it is backwards looking and is often a form-filling exercise which carefully avoids talking about what is important. There are several ways of discovering worthwhile feedback:

▶ Watch the feet, not the mouth. What people say is often different from how they feel, especially if their feelings are negative towards you. Their body language and their actions will say more about how positive they really feel than their words. While body language and actions may display the symptoms of discomfort, they give no clue as to the causes of discomfort. For that, you have to dig further.

▶ Listen to what is not being said. Listening to informal feedback is like listening to a real estate agent's pitch: you are being told what they think you want to hear. What you really want to hear is what is not being said. This means you have to know what you want to find out about and then ask directly. Often, you can pair off strengths: if someone says you are good at one thing, then you might want to find out how you fare on its opposite number. For instance:

  ▷ team work versus leadership
  ▷ analytical skills versus interpersonal skills
  ▷ initiative versus dependability
  ▷ creativity versus detail
  ▷ presentation skills versus listening skills
  ▷ entrepreneurial zeal versus administrative competence.

▶ Use a coach. A good coach will be able to see things you cannot see simply by having a different and more objective perspective. They will then help you discover the new perspective for yourself so that you own it, believe in it and can act on it.

There is more to self-awareness than understanding how you affect other people. You also have to understand your own strengths and weaknesses. In theory, you will get this from all the feedback you receive. Alternatively, look at all the different jobs you see in your organisation. There are probably quite a few you would not want to do, under nearly any circumstances. Think about what turns you off those jobs: this will give you some insight of things you are not good at and do not enjoy. And you have already taken the first step to managing those weaknesses: you are letting someone else take care of them.

Typically, it makes sense to focus on your strengths and work around weaknesses. Bizarrely, many HR policies do the opposite: they are still geared up to addressing weaknesses, which are couched in the saccharine sweet language of 'development opportunities'. No one in their right mind wants to develop their weaknesses. Handle weaknesses by:

▶ Getting other people to handle your weak spots for you: if you are lousy at accounting, rest assured that there are many excellent people out there who can help.

▶ Working in a context which plays to your strengths, not to your weaknesses.

3 Self-adjustment

Self-awareness by itself is useless unless you can do something about it. There are three elements to consider:

1   control your own emotions
2   be adaptable
3   learn and grow.

1 Control your own emotions

Some of the worst professional moments come from dealing with emotional people: the person who breaks down in tears in the middle of a board presentation, or starts throwing things around in anger. It is bad to have to deal with situations like that: it is worse to be the person in tears or throwing things. From a professional point of view, we need to control our emotions. Personally, it helps to be in some control of how we feel and how we act.

Some people seem to waltz easily through life. But for most of us, life is something of a roller-coaster ride: occasional dizzying highs are mixed with a headlong rush into lows mixed with the considerable tedium of time spent waiting for the roller-coaster to start. Events clearly affect how we feel. Amidst these events it is hard to recognise that we are responsible for our own emotions. My anger, fear, frustration, joy and hope are mine. I can choose to feel that way or I can choose to feel differently. Making such choices requires a degree of Zen-like detachment which it is hard to summon up in the heat of battle. Learning such control takes time, help and practice but is a worthwhile investment personally and professionally. There are many resources out there, from training events and psychologists to life coaches and Buddhist retreats. Choose whatever works for you. The critical insight is that you can choose to feel how you want to feel. Learn to make good choices.

2 Be adaptable

The more successful managers become, the less adaptable they become. The really successful managers can often become arrogant and pig-headed. Successful managers have typically learned a formula which works for them. They eventually acquire a ten-, 20 or 30-year track record which shows that their formula works. Unless they are serious adrenalin junkies, they will not abandon a proven success formula and try something completely new. Most successful people get stuck in their ways. This can happen very early. Dealing with a range of young, and very rich, financial traders for a charity was illuminating. The traders were convinced that because they were good at trading, they knew everything about disadvantaged communities as well. They wanted to apply their trading techniques to rundown urban areas. It was a nightmare.

It takes a little humility (which is in short supply in financial trading rooms) to recognise that success is contextual. What works here today may not work elsewhere tomorrow: board rooms and class rooms are not the same.

In a subtler way, most managers will find that the rules of success and survival slowly change over the course of their careers. The rules change at different levels of the organisation and as the organisation itself changes. To survive, you have to be able to adapt to different rules and roles, situations, contexts and people.

3 Learn and grow

The Bambara are the leading tribe in Mali. An elder sat down and explained the rhythm of life for all Bambara: 'The first 20 years are about learning, the next 20 years are about doing and the last 20 years are about teaching the next generation.' There was a timeless simplicity about his explanation of life which was well adapted to the timeless and unchanging seasonal cycles in Mali.

In an unchanging world we can, perhaps, leave learning behind after the first 20 years of our lives. Our world is changing faster than ever before, and in future it will change faster still. The half-life of most knowledge is shrinking rapidly. We have to keep learning, just to stay still relative to everyone else.

Learning comes in two major flavours, with many variants of each flavour:

1 *Explicit knowledge and learning.* This is what education is normally about: 'Know what' topics. Most managers feel comfortable learning in this area. It is not a sign of weakness for a marketing executive to go on an introduction to accounting, or for an accountant to go on an introduction to marketing. Finance, strategy, organisation design and IT all fit comfortably into the explicit knowledge box, and there are plenty of reliable suppliers who can package and present such knowledge.

2 *Tacit knowledge, or know-how.* Many managers have a blind spot about learning tacit knowledge. All training presumes a deficit: it makes up for something we are less than brilliant at. Going on a course about influencing, motivating or coaching implies that we are not good at influencing, motivating or coaching. Given that these are core management tasks, most managers do not care to admit that they are less than perfect in these areas. Casual observation of most offices is enough to dispel such complacency. Tacit knowledge needs to be learned and refreshed with at least as much diligence as explicit knowledge.

3.8 Using time effectively: activity versus achievement

Time is our most valuable resource. We have a limited amount of time, which ultimately runs out. We all have a use by date in our careers and lives. There are only three ways in which we can make the most of this limited resource:

1 Delegate: get other people to do things and save our time for other matters.

2 Be efficient in what we do: do things the right way.

3 Be effective in what we do: do the right thing.

Delegation has already been covered in section 3.4. If we cannot delegate well, then we will rapidly run out of time and we will fail the most basic test of management: we will be unable to make things happen through other people.

After delegating what we can, we are left with efficiency and effectiveness.

Time efficiency

Much of the modern world is obsessed with time efficiency: we want to do everything faster and to multi-task at the same time. We are desperately trying to squeeze a quart of activity into a pint pot of time. But there is a paradox here. The more we use the time and labour-saving devices, the more stressed and time starved we become. Technology does not free us: it enslaves us.

There is a simple resolution of the time paradox. Time and labour-saving devices never save time: they raise expectations.

Technology and the time paradox
Technology does not save time: it eats time by raising expectations.

Communication

Old world: Letters written by hand or typed (with plenty of correction fluid) meant that there were few letters written, but that each one was important and commanded attention. Replies were slow but equally important.

New world: Email and mobile phones mean that we are meant to be in touch 24/7, even on holiday, with rapid responses to a deluge of trivial messages which are sent out on a 'just-in-case' basis.

Result: Email and mobile phones increase the working week and stress. Information hyperinflation has made each message potentially worthless.

Transport

Old world: The boat from England to Empire, or from Rome to Judea, took weeks and was very expensive. So when people travelled, they made sure they got a serious result. And they also had to delegate. There was no time to ask for directions from Rome or London on how

---

to handle a local riot: people on the ground had to be trained and trusted to make big decisions by themselves instead of setting-up a global conference call to cover their backs in case it all went wrong.

New world: The one-day transatlantic visit is a badge of corporate honour to show how busy the executive is. It is also a sign that the local people are not seen to be able to do things by themselves.

Result: Because we can travel more, we do travel more. More stress, more jet lag and more air miles.

Presentations

Old world: Presentations were a slow and expensive nightmare, involving art departments and graphics people to prepare slides. As a result, each presentation tended to be short and concise.

New world: PowerPoint enables executives to prepare 200-page documents with lots of snazzy back-up slides without the time and expense of art and graphics departments.

Result: Executives waste time on PowerPoint, preparing presentations which are far too long. PowerPoint has raised expectations and no executive dares to be left behind. Labour has not been saved: standards have gone up.

Technology may save time, but for whom? It is always the employer, not the employee, who has to reap the benefits of increased productivity to stay competitive. Technology puts employees on a treadmill where we have to run faster and faster just to stay still. The faster we run, the faster our competitors run. We are running flat out but we are standing still compared to our competitors. Standards rise, and employees pay the price of meeting those standards.

Not all technology saves time. *Personnel Today* (June 2005), found that male workers spend an average of four hours a day surfing the Internet for personal reasons, and female workers spend 2.5 hours a day surfing. Even allowing for the unreliability of all such surveys, most of us will recognise that the Internet is as much a time user as a time saver.

If technology will not save our time, we need to find some more, old-fashioned ways of maximising personal efficiency.

Do it right first time, every time

Rework is a time killer. It can more than double the time taken for a task. Rework means more than doing the work again. Unpicking work can be very time consuming. It means trying to find out where things went wrong in the first place; renegotiating with people who were involved in the early work and trying to re-establish personal credibility and authority. To do it right first time means slowing down in order to speed up. Slowing down is about planning work carefully at the start; negotiating and checking expectations with key stakeholders before starting and then checking progress at regular intervals to avoid misunderstandings later. Like the slow tortoise which moves purposefully forwards, you can beat the hare that runs in circles.

Handle each communication once

Half-doing a job is as bad as doing it wrong: both result in unnecessary rework. In the case of communications, unanswered phone calls and emails simply add to the mental log jam of stuff which clutters things up. It is an unwanted distraction. There are four ways of dealing with most communications: do it, delegate it, defer it or ditch it. In order of priority, they are:

▶ *Ditch it.* File in the number one file: the waste bin. Avoid getting sucked into fruitless activity by responding to the most insidious form of junk mail – email from colleagues who copy everyone in on everything. The waste bin is the busy executive's best friend.

▶ *Delegate it.* Push the communication back to the sender, or onto someone else, for action. Ensure the recipient knows why they are receiving the communication and what action they are expected to take.

▶ *Do it.* Most emails and phone calls can be dealt with immediately ('yes, I will forward that report to you; no, I cannot come to that meeting'). Use the three-minute rule: if you can do it in three minutes, do it and get it out of the way.

▶ *Defer it.* If more work is required, be clear about what will happen and by when. This then becomes an item to sort out in your overall priorities (time effectiveness is discussed below). As this is now an addition to your workload, the defer it option is the least attractive of the four options.

Some non-actionable items may contain useful information. Note it, file it, move on.

Do it now: avoid procrastination

Classic symptoms of procrastination are displacement activities. Instead of doing the job, people do something else like surfing the web, having a coffee, gossiping or doing a minor task. The causes of procrastination will be some combination of:

▶ *Wrong time of day*: our energy levels go up and down over the day. Find easy tasks to do when energy levels are low and tackle the harder stuff when your energy levels are up and when you are least likely to be distracted by other people and issues.

▶ *Job too difficult or ambiguous*: the hardest jobs are the easiest to delay. Break a large job down into bite-sized chunks so that you do not get indigestion even thinking about the problem. It is easier to see progress and feel motivated by tackling a series of small tasks than trying to tackle one huge problem. Like climbing a mountain, it is best done one small step at a time rather than attempting one big leap.

▶ *Perfectionism*: waiting for the perfect conditions or the perfect outcome is as fruitless as *Waiting for Godot* (Samuel Becket's play). The perfect is the enemy of the good. Find an acceptable start and end point. The important thing is to move to action and do what you can, rather than worry about what you cannot do. If you worry about what you cannot do or control, you will never stop worrying and never achieve anything.

▶ *Confusion*. Lack of clarity around goals and how to get there can lead to rabbit in headlights syndrome: the executive is frozen. Ask for help and guidance from the boss: get out of the headlights before the deadlines run you over.

▶ *Chaos* comes in two versions. The first version is physical chaos of papers strewn all over the desk. Each person needs to find their own preferred working environment, but chaos is rarely effective. The second version of chaos is chaos around priorities, which leads straight back to the rabbit in headlights syndrome.

Time effectiveness

Time-efficient managers can be spotted everywhere. They are at the airport, talking on their phone while writing emails on their laptops. They can be spotted bumping into people on the street as they play with their highly addictive Crackberries. Whether they are achieving anything is another matter. Many executives make the fundamental mistake of confusing activity with achievement. At year end, however, it is achievement and not activity which counts for bonus and promotion.

Time efficiency is about doing things the right way. Time effectiveness is about doing the right things. Being 100 per cent perfect at doing the wrong thing is still a 100 per cent waste of time. The real management challenge is to do the right things. Doing the right thing is a mixture of three elements:

1　Knowing what you want to achieve

2　Focusing on important stuff

3　Dealing with the urgent stuff.

Charles Darwin: activity versus achievement

Charles Darwin had all the appearances of a leisured toff. Reading his account of the three-year voyage of the Beagle is a revelation. He did not spend most of his time at sea or in scientific pursuits. He spent most of his time on land, visiting friends of friends in places like Argentina and having a very agreeable time. He was, by modern standards, wasting his time completely.

But he was not completely idle. He famously collected and studied different varieties of finches in the Galapagos and was baffled by their slightly different beaks. He continued to think about this after his return to England. He was a geologist by training and thought only as a geologist can think: in the millions of years which enable the sea bed to rise into mountains. With that sort of time he could imagine how animals could adapt and change dramatically. Slowly, he formulated the idea of evolution.

Darwin may have been idle by modern standards, but he was also focused. Being focused, he achieved far more than all the stressed out, multi-tasking 24/7 executives who are busy being important. Activity and achievement are very different concepts.

---

1 Knowing what you want to achieve

Not all of us will have the chance to transform one of the sciences. But if we want to be effective with our time, we should think carefully about what we want to achieve. There are no simple answers, but there are some simple questions. These are deeply irritating questions to be asked when the flak is flying. They are questions to think about at quiet moments away from the pressures of work.

- When (if) I retire, what will I tell my grandchildren I did?
- In ten (20) years' time, how will I remember this year?
- What are my goals for this year? Quarter? Month? Week? Day? Hour? Now?
- Are my activities now consistent with my answers to the first three questions?
- How can I create or find a context which allows me to achieve what I want in the first three questions?

Here are some things you will not remember in 20 years' time:

- the number of emails sent, phone calls made or meetings attended
- your year-end bonus or pay rise
- your performance against your official targets
- time spent in the office or on the road.

These, however, are exactly the sorts of things which consume most management time and attention on a daily and annual basis. The point about them is that they are not ends in themselves: they are means to an end. Emails, meetings and phone calls are all essential activities, but they are only relevant if they lead to achieving something meaningful – both professionally and personally. Even beating this year's sales target is not an end in itself: it is a means to some other professional or personal goal. Personally it pays the bills and may help fund some long-held desire; professionally, beating sales targets is perhaps just a stepping stone to getting that job or starting that organisation which you have always wanted.

Knowing what you want to do sounds obvious, but it is not. In George Orwell's words: 'To see what is in front of your nose requires constant struggle.' Many executives fail to see what is in front of their noses. Immediate challenges blind them to other opportunities. Occasionally, a sideways move to build experience, skills and networks offers a better way of achieving long-term goals than mindless focus on goals mandated from above. The courage to move sideways only comes from knowing what you are looking for.

2 Focusing on the important stuff

The typical management day is crammed with urgent items. The daily flood of emails and phone calls threaten to drown us if we do not deal with them. But the risk is that urgent matters crowd out important matters. The short term always takes priority over the long term. The problem with this approach is that at some point the long term becomes short term and what could have been handled easily suddenly becomes a crisis.

There are three simplistic solutions to this, which in some circumstances can work:

1   Deal with matters which are both important and urgent first. The problem with this is that not all important things are urgent. Aged 65, people discover pensions are important and urgent. At age 25 they may still be seen as important but they are not urgent so they are ignored: welcome to an impoverished old age.

2   Set aside time in the day to progress important matters and allow no distraction from urgent matters. This is a solution favoured by time-management gurus who do not have to live the reality of management: shutting out the external world is not a viable option for many managers.

3   Delay working on matters which are not important. The problem is that even unimportant things need to happen. If you build a computer, ordering the high-value processors is clearly very important. Ordering the low-value Styrofoam packaging seems much less important, until you try shipping the computer without it. Just because something appears unimportant does not make it unnecessary. It still has to be done.

The problem with many important agenda items is that they are also the most complicated, most time-consuming and longest lead-time items. Often, is not possible to deal with them by locking the door and shutting out urgent matters for an hour or two. The more practical answer is to break the big task down into smaller bite-sized tasks, as outlined above. Even if you cannot find two hours in the day to deal with important matters, you can find a few minutes in which to have a critical conversation with someone, to check a few facts or to ask for some advice.

With important and difficult matters, thinking ahead pays big dividends. Work back from the desired end result and identify the critical path for getting there. This allows you to start things early and avoid time-consuming crises later. Start the analysis early; find out early what the approval mechanisms are; get advice, direction and support early; do some early tests. All of these things help shape and focus later work which will save time. It also means that when, inevitably, there is a setback it does not automatically become a crisis around deadlines. You have spare time and do not need to get stressed out.

Time management and the cookie jar

Try this experiment. Take a large cookie jar. Put some large stones in it until there is no more space.

No more space? Put some small pebbles until there is no more space between the stones.

No more space? Try pouring in some sand around the pebbles, so that there really is no more space.

No more space? Pour in some water, until it is at the top of the cookie jar. Now it really is full.

Now think of your day. The large stones are the really important things you must achieve. Put them into your day first and work on them. In the spaces between your important stones, you can fit in a few things you really want to do (the pebbles). In between all the pebbles are the sand and the water: these are the small but irritating things you have to do anyway, like answering emails, which can be fitted into any small spare slots in the day.

Queues and delays were invented specially for dealing with emails and phone calls which would otherwise get in the way of dealing with the important stones in your day. The cookie jar test is a simple way of making sure you deal with the important stuff, not just the urgent and routine stuff. You can as easily fill a cookie jar with sand and water as you can fill your day with urgent and routine stuff: do not let it take over and prevent you dealing with the important stuff.

Time management comes down to observing a few simple, practical, obvious and even boring disciplines as follows:

▶ Create your personal list of long-term (five-year-plus) goals. Three goals at most: one goal is better. Then look long and hard at how you will get there and how well your current situation meets your needs. To avoid death by list mania, these are goals which are often best kept in your head.

▶ Create your list of goals for this year. A good list will have the following characteristics:

  ▷ It will be short: perhaps three professional and three personal goals.

  ▷ The professional goals should fit with what your boss expects: negotiate if you can.

  ▷ Personal goals should align with your professional goals. Perhaps you want to acquire some skills or develop some new options from within your current work.

  ▷ Goals are not just financial and numeric: they can be about skills, people, life and family events.

  ▷ Test your annual goals against the 20-year rule: if I achieve these goals, will I remember this year in 20 years' time? If you forget a year, you have lost a year of your life.

▶ Create your list of goals for this month and this week. The weekly goals list is a quick exercise for Sunday evening. The weekly list will:

  ▷ distinguish between important and urgent items, as described above.

  ▷ support achievement of the monthly and annual goals.

> break down the important items into bite-sized chunks which can be dealt with piecemeal over the course of the week.

▶ Create your to do list for tomorrow. Do your best to schedule the day into three major chunks:

> Committed time. These are, for example, obligatory meetings. Review them in advance to see how you can use them to progress your important agenda items. The formal meeting may not help, but it may create the opportunity for an informal conversation with a difficult-to-find colleague.

> Urgent matters. This ensures that urgent items are not dropped and do not become crisis items. Find a time of day when you enjoy dealing with this sort of stuff. Often, first thing in the day is when people are freshest and can deal with matters fast.

> Important matters. Think ahead. Buy time by getting a head start on long lead time items. Do not worry about doing it all: focus on what you can do now, not on what you cannot do. Do not seek the perfect solution, seek to make progress. If you try to hit a hole in one, you will waste time. Get your putter out and hit the ball a few feet toward the flag, even if it is 450 yards away. You may need rather a lot of shots, but you will have got to the hole faster than the person on the tee who is still trying for the hole in one.

There is one more tip for time management: once you have made all your lists, act on them.

3 Dealing with the urgent stuff

Urgent stuff may be unimportant and irritating. No one needs that request from a senior manager for an urgent reworking of a standard report into some custom analysis which is nearly impossible to perform. But management reality is that if the urgent stuff is not dealt with, it rapidly becomes a crisis. Dealing with urgent stuff has already been dealt with, in effect, in the section above on time efficiency. The key principles are:

▶ Do it right first time, every time.

▶ Handle each task once: complete it while you can by doing it, delegating it or ditching it. (Challenge whether the urgent custom analysis really needs to be fully customised: perhaps just one essential piece of information is needed.)

▶ Do it now: avoid procrastination.

3.9 Surviving the management marathon: from days to decades

In days long gone, becoming a senior manager was like joining a club. The reserved parking space, separate dining rooms, the management floor, special elevators, the country club privileges and a nine to five existence while the workers toiled on your behalf. Now things have reversed. The workers stick to their 40-hour week (35 in France) and live a life of relative leisure: they leave work at work. Now it is the managers who have to toil in a 24/7, do-it-now, make-it-happen world of non-stop paranoia. Somewhere along the line things went wrong and management became seriously hard work.

Inevitably, there has been a backlash. An entire industry has mushroomed into existence claiming to solve the problems of burn-out and stress. The gurus of this industry have a mad glint in their eyes: they have become true believers in their new religion. They have all the smugness of people who have worked out what they want and are determined to inflict their solutions on the rest of us. They are missionaries spreading the word of wellness. Some managers are converted and get the mad glint in their eyes too. Many others feel their skin crawl as the preachers turn up to make their pitch. What the preachers say and what the managers hear are completely different things:

Preacher says	Manager thinks
Work–life balance	Preacher wants an excuse to work less: what a loser
Spirituality	Pass the *Kool Aid* – I'm expected to do something insanely stupid
Downshifting	Preacher's giving up to start a vegan farm in Vermont
Well-being	Preacher's going to make us all hug each other
Stress management	Preacher needs more stress, not less: perhaps I will provide some now

There are three problems here:

1   Stress and burn out are real.

2   Going on stress/wellness courses is seen as a sign of weakness: only wimps need attend.

3   Many of the solutions are very poor.

Real managers need real solutions: a way of living with the demands of management for decades rather than ducking out to start that vegan farm in Vermont. As ever, it pays to understand the problem before providing the solution.

Stress and the challenge of the management marathon

Most of the literature and the gurus regard stress as a Bad Thing. This is nonsense. Within reason, stress is very useful. Think for a moment about which sort of conditions bring out the best in you:

▶ The chill-out environment: undemanding work and deadlines; creative zones with funky chairs and whale music; and an understanding employer who provides generous holidays, team building events, celebrations and concierge services. Nice place to work.

▶ The work-out environment: demanding work, deadlines, bosses and clients with not quite enough resource. Constant challenge and struggle with limited resources: focus on achievement and outcomes. Life beyond the comfort zone.

For most people, the work-out environment will bring out the best in them. They are being stretched, without being broken. This is the ideal performance zone. The problem with stress is when you go into overload and reach the break-down zone (see the zone diagram). At this stage the remedy is not to go back to the stretch zone: you need to rebuild confidence in the comfort zone again before starting to stretch. It pays to recognise this and act accordingly both with yourself and with your team.

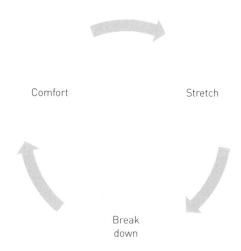

Comfort   Stretch

Break
down

The zone diagram

At first it seems odd that people put themselves into positions where they are going to be outside their comfort zones and feel stressed. A cursory glance at the top graduate employers in most countries show that the most popular employers are also the ones which generate the greatest amount of stress: banks and consulting firms lead the way. Far from avoiding stress, top graduates actively seek out stressful environments. Having interviewed several hundred graduates for an hour each, some patterns become clear in this behaviour. Graduates seek the high-stress employers because they:

- ▶ enjoy the prestige of being with what is perceived to be a top firm: they gain bragging rights with family and friends
- ▶ want to work with a peer group of equals, even though that means competition for promotion is far more intense than elsewhere
- ▶ want to gain experience which will help them build their careers longer term

▶ are slightly naïve about the real scale of the challenge they face

▶ enjoy the buzz of a dynamic and exciting organisation and peer group.

You do not have to be an adrenalin junkie to want to work in a high-performing organisation with high-performing peers. Stress is simply a by-product of such a desire. Highly demanding jobs are not the preserve only of banks and consulting firms: teaching in challenging inner city schools (Teach First and Teach for America), becoming a junior hospital doctor or signing up for the armed forces all provide highly demanding environments which are very attractive to top graduates. Top managers do not avoid stress or seek to minimise it: they actively seek out stressful situations which are personally rewarding.

Ultimately, people go into stressful situations because they enjoy them. This is smart thinking. You only excel at what you enjoy. No leading sportsman dislikes his sport, even though he suffers setbacks and losses. Equally, no successful manager dislikes her business, even though she too suffers setbacks and losses. The right amount of stress helps people reach out of their comfort zone to improve their performance. Stress, in the right quantities, should be embraced, not avoided.

Walking, running and dying

Sarah had been poached from a rival electronics retailer. She would be a good source of competitive intelligence, so I decided to debrief her on her experiences.

Jo: 'What is the biggest difference between this organisation and your last one?'

Sarah: 'People walk here.'

Jo: '???'

Sarah: 'At my last place, no one walked. We never had time. We ran to meetings. If we heard the phone ring, we ran to pick it up within three rings. It was a constant rush. Very demanding, but with a real buzz.'

Jo: 'And here?'

> Sarah: 'We walk. People let the phone ring unanswered. It does not bother them. There is plenty of time for everything. I have moved from a running organisation to a walking organisation. It is much easier here.'
>
> Within three years the walking organisation was out of business, out run and overtaken by the running organisation. My next assignment was neither a running nor a walking organisation: it was a sleeping organisation. Being part of government, it is still in business.

The problems start when stress becomes excessive and managers leave the stretch zone and enter the breakdown zone. All managers find themselves testing these limits and going too far. We cannot know our limits until we have exceeded them. Below is a checklist of the symptoms of excessive stress. Be careful when you look at the list: it is like reading a medical dictionary and discovering that you have the symptoms of every single disease known to man. Hypochondria and paranoia quickly follow. Most managers will experience most of these symptoms at some stage: that is normal. You have to decide for yourself whether the symptoms have become big enough to be dysfunctional and are affecting your performance. If this happens, a death spiral starts: increased stress leads to worse performance which leads to more stress which leads to even worse performance.

Checklist of excessive stress

The major symptoms of excessive stress include:

1 Increased irritability: short fuse
2 Lower levels of physical and emotional energy
3 Increased frustration with the job and with colleagues
4 More negative thinking: sense of the impossible, not the possible
5 Obstacles loom large: molehills become mountains
6 Feeling of being overloaded and out of control
7 Increased use of alcohol, tobacco, caffeine and drugs
8 Increased weight
9 Decreasing amounts of exercise
10 Poor and disrupted sleep patterns.

If this looks familiar, it is worth taking stock and finding some solutions. A good start is a visit to your family doctor. Beyond that, there are some tried and tested managerial remedies: not all of them work for all people. You have to try different strategies and discover which ones work best for you.

There are four types of strategy for sustaining the management marathon:

1   Regain control.

2   Rest.

3   Relax.

4   Reflect.

1 Regain control

Much stress comes from being in situations which we cannot control but are important to us. If we can regain control of the situation, we start to reduce our stress levels. Humans prefer to be in control of their destiny. We can regain control both at a tactical level and at a strategic one.

Tactically, regaining control requires taking stock of the current situation. Review the current challenges and assign them an ABC ranking:

A   Important items which I can do something about: I may not be able to address the entire item, but there are a few things I can start to make progress on. Finding the early wins, building a little momentum can quickly restore confidence both personally and with your colleagues. Focus on the few things you can do, not on the many things you cannot do.

B   Items which are important and where I need help. The help may be in clearing a political log jam, clarifying goals, re-ordering priorities. Do not let the confusion and anxiety build up. Be proactive and seek a resolution, probably with the boss. The positive approach is to talk about priorities (which is a positive spin on reducing the immediate workload) and goal clarity and focus (which is a positive spin on sorting out confusion).

C   Items which are less important that I can ditch, delay or delegate. Be ruthless in eliminating as much noise and junk from your to do list: you will probably need to focus all your energies on the A-list items.

The ABC approach is about gaining control, moving to action and rebuilding confidence. It requires focus on the things you can do (even if there are not many of them) and getting help on items where you do not have control.

Strategically, regaining control requires finding an environment where you can succeed without excessive stress. This may be another post within the same organisation or in another organisation. There is little point in living in a death spiral of increasing stress and decreasing performance. Professionally, the cost is a wrecked career. Personally, the cost is a wrecked family.

2 Rest

If someone comes into work having drunk three pints of beer for breakfast, they would probably be fired on the spot. If someone comes into work having slept for just a couple of hours a night for three nights in a row, they get to wear a badge of corporate valour for their commitment and dedication. Jet lag is cool for the hyper-busy executive. In practice, they too should be fired. In tests, the reaction times and decision-making capabilities of the drunk and the sleep-deprived executive are the same. Both have made themselves into liabilities to their employers.

Sleeping in Brussels

Thursday was D Day: we had to pitch a big new idea to the board. At 8pm, the presentation looked good, so I went to the hotel and slept. The team was really dedicated: team members stayed up until 2am working and reworking the presentation. At 6.30am they were back in the war room again.

At 7.30am I rolled up. I nearly felt guilty that the team members had decided to stay up even though I had encouraged them to get a good night's sleep. Their faces were white with exhaustion. I felt pretty good. They asked if they could now produce the presentation which they had revised overnight. I looked at it. It had steadily gone backwards from 8pm the previous evening. The fine-tuning added lots of clever detail, but destroyed the logic flow and simplicity of the original. I let them produce the presentation: the 8pm version. They were devastated.

At 10am, we presented. The pitch was simple, and it was familiar. The client loved it and we landed up working there for another 18 months. Doing less (well) is better than doing more (poorly).

The more stressful situations become, the more important it is to sleep well. This is counter intuitive. Most managers intuitively work longer in stressful situations. The better solution is to work effectively for a shorter period than to work ineffectively for a longer period. Sleep deprivation is not the high road to effective working.

3 Relax

Relaxation techniques range from the weird and whacky to the dangerous, with a few useful ones in between. The important thing is to know how to relax and to decompress. Even on holiday, it is easy to spot the hyped-up manager who is still in command, control and compete mode. Symptoms of the unrelaxed manager on holiday include:

- urgently organising friends and family, even though they would organise themselves quite happily
- barking demands and complaints at hapless receptionists, waiters and check-in staff
- itching to get back on to email and the mobile phone, just in case something is happening back at the office
- boasting to all who will listen about their exotic travels, demanding work and high-maintenance lifestyle.

These people are a pain to be with on holiday. They are also a pain at work and a pain to themselves. To be effective, managers need to vary their pitch and pace. If they are always working in command, control and compete mode, three consequences follow:

1   Colleagues tune out.
2   The manager raises the pitch and tempo even further to get heard. Colleagues get used to the increased pitch and tempo and tune that out, so the manager raises the stakes in a never ending spiral.
3   Eventually, the manager burns out.

Varying pitch and pace avoids the tune out and burn out death spiral. Relaxing helps professionally and personally. By slowing down, colleagues take more notice when the manager raises the pace and pitch. Personally, slowing down allows for decompression and recovery time, which leads to increased energy levels for the times when high pace and pitch are required.

The challenge for the stressed out executive is to know how to relax in the face of unrelenting pressures. Each person finds their own way of relaxing. Some lose themselves in music, or in the mindless tedium of running and exercise. Other relaxation techniques, such as drinking, smoking and eating to excess relieve the immediate symptoms of stress but add to the underlying problems. Choose your style of relaxation with care.

There are some classic relaxation techniques which can be deployed in the office, without running or drinking. These are described below: try them. Like all new things, they may feel odd at first. With persistence, you will find some which work. The three classic techniques are:

1   Progressive physical relaxation

2   Positive visualisation

3   Controlled breathing.

1 Progressive physical relaxation (PPR)

These are the exercises which are commonly recommended on long-haul flights. They can be done at your desk somewhat more easily than they can be done in the confines of an economy class seat. The basic idea is that if you can relax your body, you can relax your mind. You will probably have noticed that when you are very stressed and tense, your body becomes tense as well: hunched shoulders, clenched jaw and grinding teeth. Reverse these symptoms and the mind starts to unwind as well. In its simplest form, PPR requires no more than noticing the hunched shoulders and relaxing them, noticing the clenched jaw and relaxing it.

The full version of PPR starts with the toes. Wriggle them. You are even allowed to smile as you wriggle your toes, unseen by all your colleagues. Bring your toes back so that your calf muscles stretch. Rotate your ankle, get the blood moving freely. Work slowly upwards. Stretch the calf muscles again. Stretch your whole leg out beneath the table. Move onto your stomach: breathe in and out deeply and quietly. Let your stomach and chest rise and fall with each breath. By now, you should be feeling more of your body is relaxing. Sit up straight: get your backbone out of its foetus-style curl. Move up to your shoulders. Let them drop. Work your hands and fingers: stretch them and ease them. All of this can be done in a few minutes without colleagues noticing anything.

The head and neck exercises are more visible. Ease your neck by rotating your shoulders backwards and forwards; rotate your neck to ease it; work your facial muscles to ease them: silly faces and smiling are not mandatory but are a great way of removing tension, at least in private.

If you can quietly do this two or three times a day you will find that the stress evaporates as your body relaxes, and you will be much better able to deal with the crises of the normal managerial day.

2 Positive visualisation

Sport stars learn to visualise success, not failure. Visualising failure is a self-fulfilling prophecy. Managers can use the same trick. The key is knowing how to do it.

For a moment, imagine that you have a big presentation to make. Feeling nervous is natural: there is so much that can go wrong from the logistics (the projector fails) to the content, audience and your own performance. Problem focus leads to fear and anxiety. Instead, try to visualise in detail what a good scenario looks like, from the moment you walk up to start the presentation. Mentally, walk through what success looks like, how you will feel, how you will sound, what you will do and say, how people will react. Use all your senses to make the visualisation as vivid as possible: imagine the sights, sounds, smells and feel of the event. When you know exactly what success looks like, you are in a position to deliver it. If you do not know what success looks like, achieving it is little more than a lucky dip. Positive visualisation is not psychobabble: it is the routine of winners in sport and in business.

3 Controlled breathing

Controlled breathing is brought to global managers courtesy of Buddhist monks. For the monks, controlled breathing is the first step towards controlling their minds and ultimately escaping the endless cycle of birth, death and suffering. For managers, it is enough to escape the endless cycle of projects, deadlines and stress.

For monks and managers alike, the purpose of controlled breathing is to control the mind. If you can control your mind, you can control your stress and learn to relax and to focus much better. This sounds easy, but it is not. There is a basic version and there is a gold-plated version to controlled breathing.

The basic version is very basic: take a few deep breaths. Let the shoulders relax. As you breathe out, blow away your stress.

The gold-plated version will not get you to Enlightenment, but it will get you to a better place than stressville. The sequence goes like this:

▶ Focus intently on breathing.

▶ Let your mind relax as it focuses on breathing.

▶ Start to observe your mind: it has a mind of its own.

▶ As you observe your mind, see how it chooses to feel: happy or stressed, relaxed or rushed.

▶ As you detach from and observe these emotions, you see how they can be made into conscious choices, not automatic and subconscious reactions of the mind.

▶ Now you can start to control your feelings: you can choose to feel more relaxed or more stressed.

▶ As you master this process, you can control your mind without the need for the preparatory breathing exercises: you have become the master of your mind and your feelings.

The key step is the first one: focus intensely on your breathing. For this you need a quiet and private space where you will not be disturbed. Sit comfortably with your back straight: a full lotus position is unhelpful for most because it is painful. Relax the body. Focus on your breathing. Observe your diaphragm rising and falling with each breath. Feel the cool air coming in over your upper lip and the warm air coming out again. As you observe and feel each breath, other thoughts are crowded out. First, the mind starts to relax; then you can start to observe it as it plays its games of worry and stress. Observe, detach and then control. Monks may take years perfecting this. For managers, a few minutes are enough to get started. After a while, you will be able to do a version of this exercise while standing on trains, waiting in queues or sitting at meetings. It is quiet, discrete and very calming.

4 Reflect

Managers know that in business you can only control what you measure. The same is true personally. If you do not measure how you feel, you are unable to control how you feel: you will have no data to show you when and why you feel good or bad.

There are three simple ways of reflecting:

1   Use a coach to help you reflect and learn.

2   Keep a stress diary: record both up moments and down moments and what caused them. Work to find situations which produce more up than down moments.

3   Keep a peace of mind chart (as in the example below).

My peace of mind chart	Weeks							
Important things to me	1	2	3	4	5	6	7	8
State of my project	7	7	6	2	2	5	7	9
Relations with boss	6	6	6	1	1	3	5	6
Relations with family	7	7	7	2	8	8	8	7
Level of exercise	8	8	3	1	6	8	7	7
Level of drinking and eating	7	7	7	3	5	7	5	7
Amount of sleep	8	8	4	2	6	8	8	8
Overall	43	43	33	11	28	39	40	44

You can make your own peace of mind chart. Fill the left-hand column with those things which seem to be most important to your personal state of well-being, and then score yourself against them regularly: weekly should be enough. Use as many rows as seem relevant. Soon you will see the patterns of what helps or hinders you.

In the example above the pattern is clear: lack of sleep and exercise is an early warning sign of impending crisis. Getting sleep and exercise back on track is the first step to recovery, along with family support. When things go wrong professionally, things go wrong personally and misery for everyone ensues. Each person will have their own distinct pattern of what is important and what works. The simple act of keeping the peace of mind chart is cathartic. It enables you to reflect and recover by putting things into perspective.

In addition to reflecting on what you do, reflect on how, where and when you do it. Different times of day may suit you for dealing with urgent trivia versus longer-term projects, or for dealing with people versus paper. Know what works best when. Reflect on your working environment. You do not need to be a believer in feng shui to realise that working conditions affect your state of mind. Simple things such as opening a window, adjusting the heating or lighting, changing chairs or rearranging the furniture can make a big difference. The Hawthorne experiments (Western Electric Company, Chicago, 1924–33 under the direction of Elton Mayo of Harvard Business School) showed that the simple act of varying conditions can lead to improved performance. Ideal conditions may not exist, but gaining control and adjusting conditions can help.

3.10 Learning the right behaviours: what managers really want

Read the literature carefully and you will discover that the ideal manager has the following characteristics and behaviours:

- ambitious and humble
- empowering and directing
- supporting and controlling
- task focused and people focused
- big picture and detailed
- intuitive and logical
- goal centred and process sensitive
- analytically rigorous and emotionally in touch

▶ entrepreneurial and reliable

▶ fast moving and methodical.

Some managers feel they already have all these qualities and many more besides. They are arrogant and dumb enough not to feel the need to read this or any other book which might make them more effective. The rest of us feel small when measured against such demanding and contradictory criteria.

At this point it made sense to ask managers what they expected of their peers, bosses and team members. Here are the results, with the criteria ranked by order. The figures in parentheses are the percentage of managers who are satisfied with the performance of their peers against the chosen criteria.

Top leaders	Leaders in the middle	Recent graduates/ emerging leaders
Vision (61%)	Ability to motivate others (43%)	Hard work (64%)
Ability to motivate others (37%)	Decisiveness (54%)	Proactivity (57%)
Decisiveness (47%)	Industry experience (70%)	Intelligence (63%)
Ability to handle crises (56%)	Networking ability (57%)	Reliability (61%)
Honesty and integrity (48%)	Delegation (43%)	Ambition (64%)

Source: Teach First/Monitor Group survey

Take a moment to review the list. Five key themes emerged from the survey:

1 The rules of survival and success change at each level of an organisation. This helps explain why people can succeed at one level and fail at the next. They have not suddenly become ineffective; they have found that a tried and tested success formula at one level does not work at the next.

2 Charisma and inspiration are notably absent from the list. This is a good thing. You cannot learn charisma or have a charisma transplant. They are not necessary. In the thousands of managers interviewed or surveyed, we found many effective individuals but few, if any, were

truly charismatic. Managerial effectiveness does not require charismatic inspirational skills.

3　The expectations are additive: senior managers are expected to have all the qualities of new, middle and senior managers. They cannot abandon intelligence, hard work or reliability as soon as they are promoted into middle management. The performance bar rises at each level of the organisation.

4　Satisfaction with managers against the criteria outlined above is, at best, average. Satisfaction levels are indicated by the percentages in brackets after each criterion. This is very good news for managers. It means that by acquiring the skills and behaviours outlined above, managers can stand out from their peers.

5　Honesty and integrity was extremely divisive. Senior managers were either rated highly or poorly: few rated average. Managers who were rated well on honesty and integrity tended to be rated well on other criteria. Managers who were rated poorly on honesty and integrity were slammed on all the other criteria: a breakdown in trust was a killer in terms of perceptions.

Honesty in investment banking

Investment banking is widely regarded as a shark pool. The leaders of investment banks should, therefore, be the biggest and meanest sharks in the pool. To discover whether this was true, I decided to interview some sharks.

Chris talked about the chairman of the investment bank:

'His defining characteristic is honesty. He never has a bad word to say about anyone. If you have a private conversation with him, you know it will stay private. He will not bad mouth anyone behind their backs. If you waste his time or you are an idiot, the only negative consequence is that you will not get another meeting with him.'

'Because of his honesty, everyone trusts him. Staff trust him. Clients trust him. This makes him very powerful in the market. Clients need people they can trust on very sensitive matters. Within the bank, he has virtually no enemies. His position is unassailable.'

Honesty and integrity has nothing to do with feeble ethics courses. It is much more important than that: it is about survival and success. Without honesty and integrity, there can be no trust, and no teamwork. This sort of honesty is not a politician's honesty which seems to mean: 'I am honest until you prove 100 per cent otherwise.' Management honesty is much stronger: it means total discretion and having the strength to deal with uncomfortable situations early. If a team member is underperforming, it is dishonest and a breach of trust to not deal with it until it becomes a surprise at assessment time. Team members need to know where they stand, especially when they are in the wrong place.

Take one more look at the list of managerial expectations. Most of the characteristics and skills have either been covered in this book (intelligence, decisiveness, ability to motivate, handling crises) or they are things you cannot be trained on, like hard work, ambition and industry experience.

The interviews behind the survey repeatedly came back to three themes:

1   People focus
2   Positive outlook
3   Professional behaviour.

1 People focus

This has been dealt with extensively already.

Positive outlook and professional behaviour are equally important behaviours, but slightly more elusive. Fortunately, they are behaviours which can be acquired.

2 Positive outlook

Being positive is a better way to live than being negative. Being British, this is difficult. Here, enthusiasm is a certifiable mental disorder. It may be something to do with the weather, the food and loss of empire. Brits do gloom better than they do enthusiasm.

For a manager, being negative has negative consequences:

▶ Your personal cloud of gloom will spread like a depression across the team, which picks up signals from your behaviour. Morale plummets.

▶ Negative thinking quickly becomes problem focus, leading to inaction and a sense of the impossible.

▶ Thinking negatively is a self-fulfilling prophecy: if you believe something cannot be achieved, it will not be achieved.

At the other extreme, relentlessly positive one-minute management quickly becomes insincere, superficial and irritating. 'Wow, you photocopied that piece of paper well' or 'Your desk is really neat today' may make some people feel good: to others they are patronising remarks. A surfeit of trivial compliments devalues real praise when it is really deserved.

Thinking positively is a learned reaction. When confronted with a situation, avoid the rush to (negative) judgement. Ask a few simple questions:

▶ *What is good about this situation?* Even if most of the report you are reviewing is garbage, there are bound to be some good things: identify them, note them and then encourage the author to build on the good points. Their motivation will be much higher than if you spend hours picking apart all the faults.

▶ *What can be improved?* Focus on the positive outcome. If it is a poor report, focus on what a good one will look like and be clear about how the report can be structured to achieve a good result. Solution focus is more helpful than problem focus.

▶ *What were they trying to achieve?* Understand motivations and intents and then help them find a way of achieving that outcome. If the offices are shabby, it may be because people are trying to save money which is not a mortal sin.

▶ *Is this an opportunity for me to shine?* The worse the situation, the bigger the opportunity to make a difference. If you inherit a perfect project, you cannot make a mark unless you fail. If you inherit a walking disaster, anything you do will likely be an improvement and you will look like a hero.

▶ *Is this an opportunity to make a friend?* If someone is in trouble, it is easy to judge or avoid them. If, on the other hand, you turn out to be the

Good Samaritan, you will have found an ally for the future. People remember those who helped them in time of greatest need.

Every cloud has a silver lining. Focus on the silver lining, not on the cloud. Do this 100 per cent of the time and people will start to follow your example. Your team will slowly become far more proactive, positive and effective.

High School Blues

The head teacher reflected on what had happened in her first year in charge. On arrival, she found that the students spoke 68 different mother tongues. Many were first-generation immigrants, with all the attendant problems of poverty, integration and lack of employment.

'Of course,' she said 'that is wonderful news. There is so much buzz and excitement from having such a diverse student population. And first-generation immigrants show real commitment to wanting to learn and make their mark in their new community. They are a joy to teach.'

'We had a challenge when one wing of the school was burned down by an arsonist. But that was a blessing in disguise. It released insurance money for redevelopment: that wing was getting old anyway.'

Most people would run away from such a challenging school. Where others saw problems, she only saw opportunities. Her confidence transmitted itself to staff and pupils and was reflected in both performance and appearance. She was so positive about the school being burned down I began to wonder who the arsonist had really been. . .

Acting positively flows from thinking positively. The real test of acting positively comes when you are confronted with a new and possibly challenging situation. There are typically four ways in which people react in order of frequency (from the top) and value (from the bottom):

▶ apathy

▶ analysis

▶ answers

▶ action.

The most frequent responses are the least helpful.

Apathy

This comes in the form of denial (it is not really a problem) deferral (it is not a problem yet) or delegation (it is a problem now, but for someone else). This is a natural reaction. Managers are busy enough already without having to add more items to their crowded agenda. Occasionally, denial, deferral or delegation can be the right response. But if everyone acts in the same apathetic way the organisation will quickly go nowhere. Managers who do not take responsibility are irresponsible.

Analysis

This is the favoured solution of smart people, and it is highly destructive. Analysis is a great way of avoiding action. It is also a great way to show that you are smart. By identifying all the issues and challenges you show you are clever, and you avoid taking any risk or responsibility. By the time you have identified 327 issues, risks and challenges, no one in their right mind is going to want to do anything: you have just achieved paralysis through analysis.

Answers

These are risky, because they may be wrong. But senior executives quickly identify managers who bring them problems and those who bring them solutions. Equally, teams are grateful to managers who can help them find solutions, not problems. Solution providers quickly earn trust and loyalty from peers, bosses and team members.

Action

This is clearly risky. You only know you are taking the right course of action when everyone else starts claiming responsibility for the action. If it turns out the wrong way, you will start to feel very lonely. And in many organisations, waiting for approval for action takes an eternity. The strong manager will move to action anyway: it is easier to ask forgiveness than to ask for permission in many organisations. If the essence of management is making things happen through other people, then action is the ideal response for the effective manager.

A bias for action is easy to talk about, harder to do. There are some simple ways of driving to action:

▶ Ask people what they would do. Force them to focus on outcomes and solutions. They will, collectively, often know what a sensible way forward looks like. If they identify it, they will be committed to it. They will also be relieved to be doing something, rather than just worrying.

▶ Focus on the possible, not the impossible. Break a big problem down into small chunks and find a few things you can start work on right away. Early wins give people a sense of momentum and confidence. They also buy some time while you figure out how to deal with the deeper challenges.

▶ Mind your language. Avoid problem focus: make people think in terms of problem and solution. The key phrase is 'How to. . .' For instance:

▷ Instead of 'it's too expensive' try 'how to fund this' (reducing the cost, finding more budget, etc.).

▷ Instead of 'it's too difficult' try 'how to source the skills required for this. . .'.

▷ Instead of 'operations will hate it' try 'how to build support for this across the organisation'.

This 'how to' approach sounds corny, but it works. It forces people to solve problems, not just identify them. It drives to action.

Professional behaviour

Professionalism is in danger of becoming a dirty word. The professional foul is the dirtiest and most cynical foul in sport. Professional politicians. And of course, professionals built the *Titanic* whereas an amateur built the Ark.

Within management, professionalism has become a vague word which means different things to different people. But professionalism is important both institutionally and individually. It pays to discover what it really means in your context and to act accordingly.

Institutional professionalism

For an organisation, professionalism is the unspoken code of conduct about how people are expected to behave. The formal values statement of the organisation is likely to be a useless guide to behaviour. Most values statements sound like a proxy statement for the United Nations and saving the planet. Managers are not required to save the planet. Saving their department, let alone their organisation, is quite enough.

Decoding the rules of conduct is a matter of observation. Look hard and see:

▶ Who gets promoted and why?

▶ Who gets the big bonuses and best assignments, and why?

▶ What are the war stories about people getting into trouble, and why?

Look at some specific behaviours and see how far they are praised or punished, and how far senior executives display these characteristics:

▶ risk taking versus risk aversion

▶ dress codes

▶ use of vacation and sickness entitlement

▶ style of talking: deference, humour, personal, analytical

▶ decision making and accountability: collective versus individual

▶ discussion style: argumentative versus consensual.

Managers need to understand the professional rules of the game in their organisation in order to survive, let alone succeed. These rules vary by organisation. For instance, attitudes to holidays and sickness time vary dramatically. In many American companies, it is a badge of honour to take no sickness and not all of the limited vacation allowance. If this means coming in with flu and infecting all your co-workers with flu as well, so be it: they will not take time off for flu either. In one European telco, the opposite is true. Staff are expected to take their full vacation allowance of 25–30 days a year (depending on seniority) plus all the public holidays. They are also expected to make full use of their sickness 'entitlement' of 12 days a year. When they have used 10 days, HR sends them a reminder to keep 2 days in reserve, just in case they really are sick. Vacations, holidays and sickness come to a handy 50 days a year, which can be extended by use of flexi-time or by carrying entitlement from one year to the next.

Once you have decoded the expected professional behaviours of the organisation, you have three choices:

1   Play according to the rules of the game: safe and low risk.

2   Cheat: in some organisations you are expected to circumvent the formal rules and to use your initiative. Changing the rules to your advantage tends to accelerate your career: you succeed faster or you fail faster.

3   Find a different game in a different organisation: nearly half of all graduates leave their first employer within five years in search of an environment which better suits them.

Individual professionalism

It is very easy to preach about what professionalism looks like. We all have our pet hates when it comes to unprofessional behaviour. The easiest professional rule is the Golden Rule: 'Do unto others as you would have them do unto you' (Luke, 6:31). A quick way to codify this:

▶   Write down a list of all your pet hates: how people irritate you by complaining, queue jumping, cutting across you when you speak, being late. Now avoid doing any of those things yourself.

▶   Write another list of the things people have done which you really appreciate: remembering your name, saying thank you, giving praise. Now do more of it yourself.

Personal professionalism is not simply a matter of being nice and following arcane rules of etiquette. It is about putting other people at ease and getting the most out of them. Professionalism may help others, but it is also in the manager's best self-interest.

PQ skills:

acquiring power to make things happen

In most organisations you can find smart people and you can find nice people. You can even find people who are both smart and nice. But they are not necessarily the best or most successful managers. There are plenty of smart, nice people with high IQ (intelligence quotient) and high EQ (emotional quotient) who are eking out a quiet existence in the backwaters of the organisation. They are much liked but little used. Meanwhile, people who are not as smart or not as nice seem to levitate magically upwards through the organisation to positions of ever greater power.

The missing element for the smart, nice people is PQ (political quotient) skills: political intelligence.

Political skills sound very Machiavellian. At times, they can be Machiavellian. So it is worth being clear what political skills are about and what they are not about for the practising manager.

Political skills are the skills you need to make things happen in an organisation. IQ skills are intellectual, EQ skills are interpersonal and PQ skills are about the organisation and action. To make things happen, managers need to know how to acquire and use power and resources. Once some power has been acquired, it has to be used well to acquire more power and more resources. Often, this involves using power and resources over which the manager has no direct control. In a matrix organisation this is an essential skill. Political skills are becoming more important as the traditional command and control organisation slowly disappears.

Politically intelligent managers need to acquire a range of skills and knowledge:

1 The seven key power sources: building a power base
2 Acquiring power: shining a light on the dark arts
  ▷ Where to find power
  ▷ The power network: career management
  ▷ Playing for power
3 Building power networks: becoming irreplaceable
4 Using power: setting your agenda
5 The art of unreasonable management: ruthlessness

6   Saying 'no' to your boss: surviving insanity

7   Power and integrity: from morality to survival

8   Taking control: telling stories

9   Managing change: people, not projects

10   People and change: through the valley of death.

These skills – discussed in the following sections – are not mysterious. They are readily learnable skills which most managers can acquire to help both themselves and their organisations. PQ is about power. As in Star Wars, power can be put to good use or bad use. Each manager makes his or her own decision about becoming a wannabe Jedi knight or a wannabe Darth Vader. Understanding the nature of power at least gives the manager the choice. Failure to build PQ condemns managers to becoming a welcome doormat for more politically astute managers.

We will look at each of these skills in turn but before we turn to the skills, it is worth looking at what political skills do *not* cover:

▶   Knifing your colleagues. There are ways of doing this: it can work in the short term, but in the long term it results in many enemies and very little trust. That is a tough way to build a career.

▶   Blustering your way to success. Perception management is important, but there has to be some substance behind the perception.

▶   Plotting the overthrow of your boss. If you try this, do not fail. The one unforgivable sin for a subordinate is disloyalty, and the boss has more power than you do. If you fail, you are dead meat.

4.1 The seven key power sources: building a power base

The most obvious source of power is seniority. The CEO clearly has great power. But the CEO also has limited time which means limited access for a small number of people. You may get lucky and find yourself working directly for the CEO, but usually managers have to find power in slightly more subtle ways. So, it helps to know what power looks like and where it comes from.

Power in an organisation comes from controlling or influencing seven major sources of power:

1 Money
2 Information
3 Skills
4 Customers
5 Access
6 Permissions
7 Scarce resource.

These sources of power work best when they work together. As you look through the above list, ask yourself two questions:

1 *How much of this sort of power do I have personally?* Most managers have relatively limited amounts of personal power, normally in just one or two areas. This modest base of personal power is what you can trade with other people to extend your influence and power.

2 *How well connected am I to people who have a lot of this sort of power?* This is where the power of each manager's network becomes critical. The low PQ manager will rely on his or her personal standing and power. The high PQ manager will build an internal network which gives access to all the power he or she needs to make things happen.

Building a network of power is essential. Personal power is often weak: it lasts until the next reorganisation or until someone else is hired with similar or better skills. A network is harder to destroy and has much more value to both the manager and to the organisation, for the same reason: an effective network enables a manager to make things happen. The more ambiguous and complicated the formal organisation is in terms of accountability and authority, the more valuable these informal networks become. Relying on formal decision-making frameworks is an exercise in frustration and futility. An informal but powerful network will enable the decision to be made informally and then let the formal systems and procedures catch up with reality. High PQ managers will value action over procedures.

1 Money

Cash is king. Budget power is often one of the most visible sources of power in an organisation. Other people may have the ideas, but if you have the budget you can decide which ideas proceed and which ones do not. In practice, budget power is often circumscribed in three ways:

1   Discretionary budgets are limited, even for CEOs. Most budgets are already heavily committed at the start of the year. Creating more discretionary budget requires cutting back in other areas or negotiating more budget from elsewhere.

2   Use of budgets is subject to scrutiny and approval, for instance from finance.

3   Budgets can be removed and budget-holders can be moved to new positions.

The importance of financial muscle can be seen in the corporate pecking order of functions. If there is one executive director who is featured in the press alongside the CEO, it is normally the CFO. Ford and GM should, perhaps, be led by people from engineering, design, technology , operations or even marketing. In practice, the finance functions in both organisations have become the locus of power over many decades.

2 Information

Not all information is equal. There is a hierarchy of information and power. Starting from the bottom:

- ▶ Unprocessed data have low value and are widely available.

- ▶ Information is processed data. This is where data becomes useful and dangerous. Data are used by managers in the same way lawyers use evidence: to prove their case rather than to discover the truth. Managers must be able to convert data into information fast and to shape decisions. Having access to a wide range of data early provides managers with the raw material to create useful information.

- ▶ Intelligence is information which is not widely available. Understanding customer intentions, predicting competitor moves, knowing what different business units and managers are really planning and thinking are all valuable sources of data. Senior executives tend to have low trust in the information which is presented to them: they know it is not objective, and they know that the information is being used to sell them a story. They tend to value intelligence which comes from apparently random gossip. The quality of the intelligence is directly proportional to the credibility of the individuals providing it: if they have been consistently reliable, their intelligence will be highly valued and respected. People with good sources of intelligence normally have well-cultivated networks across the organisation: see section 4.3 for building networks.

3 Skills

Marx was wrong about the revolution. The workers did not have to revolt against capitalist oppression to create a Stalinist utopia. Instead, they got skilled and got even with the owners of capital. The knowledge-intensive industries have seen a massive shift of economic power from the owners of capital to the owners of skills. In wholesale financial services, the top performers name their price. The owners of capital are forced to take a disproportionate share of the risk to sustain their returns.

Within the organisation, the power of the most skilled workers is reflected in their salaries. Inevitably, there is the small matter of supply and demand. As long as COBOL skills were in high demand and short supply, COBOL was a highly rewarded skill. As new software languages replaced COBOL and a few hundred thousand COBOL writers became available in Bangalore, the power of COBOL writers in the developed countries dived.

4 Customers

Professional service firms all follow the client rule: 'He (or she) who owns the client rules.' Owning the client is a strong form of controlling the cash. Ownership of the client gives control of the revenues which the client will produce. No client means no revenues means no work. Where a budget-holder can be reorganised out of a position of power, the client owner is much harder to shift. No firm wants to risk a revenue stream by changing a client owner and alienating the client.

5 Access

Access to power is used as leverage by people who do not have much power themselves: secretaries, junior and middle managers and administrative staff. Access comes from three main sources:

1   Diary control. Secretaries have a remarkable ability to free up diaries for some people and to close them out to others. It pays to have good working relationships with secretaries.

2   Personal relationships. Senior executives need their own networks of people at all levels of the organisation. The network will be their informal intelligence network (which gives them power at senior levels) and of informal support and help on *ad hoc* tasks. Middle managers can contribute to and benefit from being part of such networks.

3   Location. If you have an office next to a power broker, you can bump into them when necessary. If you are based in another city, you will only see them at formal events where it is difficult to build trust and intimacy.

6 Permissions

The power of permissions is most visibly seen in the great kleptocracies of the world. In a kleptocracy, government ministers suddenly appear to be brilliant investors who can make a few hundred million dollars from smart investments. This, of course, has nothing to do with them giving permission for the new mining venture, setting up the new car factory, granting the telecoms licence or approving the city centre redevelopment.

In organisations, permission power is largely negative. It is characterised by people who took Nancy Reagan's exhortation 'Just Say No' to heart. These are the people in health and safety, legal, brand 'police', quality control, audit and HR who can stop something because it does not comply with internal or external rules and regulations. They can use their negative power as possible trades for their own interests, but they have limited positive power: the ability to make things happen.

7 Scarce resource

The shape of organisations is changing. As they focus more on their core competences, they outsource more of their activities. In a virtual organisation, sourcing and control of suppliers can be as critical as sourcing and control over customers. Managers who have a good network of suppliers and understand how to manage them are valuable. Neither their networks nor their knowledge are easily replaceable.

4.2 Acquiring power: shining a light on the dark arts

Where to find power

Prospecting for power leads in two opposite directions. Both strategies work. Most managers use both strategies at different stages of their careers. Power can be found at both the:

▶ heart of the empire, and at

▶ outposts of empire.

Power at the heart of the empire

Willy Sutton, the famous American bank robber, was asked why he robbed banks. 'Because that is where the money is,' he replied. Duh. If you want money, go where the money is. If you want fun, go where the fun is. If you want power, go where the power is. This is the most obvious power strategy. Being at the heart of the empire confers huge advantages to the manager:

▶ access to informal information and knowledge

▶ access to key decision makers, informally and frequently

▶ ability to build an extended network of managers with power

▶ early sight of attractive programmes and positions

▶ visibility to senior executives

▶ insight of the organisation's real priorities and decision-making processes.

None of these insider advantages come gift wrapped waiting for you at your cubicle the day you arrive at head office. You have to work to build the informal networks and knowledge. But at least you have the opportunity to build these informal networks faster than someone in the outposts of empire who only visits head office once a quarter for a conference or an appraisal.

A cubicle in head office does not guarantee success. There are some functions and roles which carry more weight than others. In career terms, it makes sense to be where the power is. This varies by organisation, for instance:

▶ Proctor & Gamble (P&G): marketing

▶ GM and Ford: finance

▶ Dyson: design

▶ Professional service firms: clients

▶ Toyota and Nissan: engineering.

A finance person at P&G's Cincinatti head office or a marketing person at Ford's Dearborn headquarters will be close to power, but they will not have it. They will be like the beggar looking through the shop windows on Fifth Avenue: they are close to wealth, they can see the wealth, but they cannot touch the wealth. It is a frustrating experience. Power starts by making the right career choices.

Some organisations deliberately cultivate future leaders by placing them at the heart of power early in their careers. BP selects high-potential graduates to work in the CEO's office for one or two years. In that time they will learn how the organisation really works; they will build their networks of support and influence and they will start to learn how a senior executive thinks and acts. These are invaluable lessons to learn. But gaining this sort of access is unusual.

The main drawback to seeking the heart of power is competition. Your colleagues are your deadliest competitors. Managers are attracted to power like moths to a light. A short walk around any corporate headquarters is enough to find managers dancing around different light and power sources, all trying to get as close as possible to the brightest light. Inevitably, quite a few get burned in the process. Below we look at how to acquire the power once you have identified it.

Power at the outposts of empire

Going to an outpost of empire may seem like being exiled to lingering career death. Handled incorrectly, that is exactly what it is. Handled correctly, an outpost of empire is an essential stepping stone to success.

Outposts of empire are good news. A middle manager may be lost in cubicle land at headquarters where there is intense competition for attention. Managers who know their competitive strategy will recognise that the best way to win is without a fight: occupy new territory (competitive 'white spaces' in the words of Prahalad and Hamel). These outposts are often attractive career staging posts because they:

▶ Offer the chance to wield real authority: limited responsibility in an ambiguous matrix can be replaced by genuine authority and responsibility in an outpost.

▶ Offer rapid development: the manager can experiment and even fail occasionally away from the intense competition and gossip in the limelight at headquarters.

▶ Allow the manager to build a track record and build credibility: GE has many smaller business units which it calls 'lemonade stands'. These give potential general managers the chance to build and demonstrate their capabilities.

▶ Enable the manager to build a power base and an empire of his or her own: an unloved skunk works can quickly become a strategic business in its own right. IBM's PC division was an affront to an organisation which lived mainframes: it quickly moved from being an unloved orphan to a star, until it finally hollowed itself out completely and got taken over by Lenovo.

An assignment to the outposts of empire can be a one-way ticket to triumph or tragedy. To avoid the latter there are three golden rules to observe:

1 *Believe nothing.* When you negotiate your exile, you may diligently negotiate promises about what will happen on your return: the career opportunities that will be yours and the promotions available in three

years' time. Anything you agree is worthless. In three years' time, the organisation will have gone through one or two reorganisations. The openings you hoped for will have disappeared into the black hole of any reorganisation. Your boss will have changed. Your new boss will not feel deeply committed to keeping promises which he did not make and which are impossible to fulfil in the new organisation anyway. You have to make your own future, rather than relying on people to keep promises made on their behalf years ago.

2   *Stay in touch.* You have to stay on the corporate radar screen. In an outpost of empire you are cut off from the gossip, the power networks, the shifting sands of new opportunities, reorganisations and new initiatives. People forget that you exist because they no longer see you in the corridor. So make sure you find plenty of excuses to go back to the heart of empire for budget meetings, training events, corporate events. Volunteer for corporate projects which maintain your visibility and enable you to appear back in the heart of empire. Stay in touch with HR and the power brokers who will know what openings are going to appear when: make sure you manage your transition back into the corporate heart when attractive positions are opening up.

3   *Manage perceptions.* The good news about the outposts of empire is that no one in the heart of empire really understands what on earth is happening there or why. This is, of course, also the bad news. All the functionaries back in head office see are the numbers which say whether you have positive or negative variances against budget. This makes perception management essential. It also makes it essential to set the baseline as low as possible at the start of the year so that all the functionaries see positive variances for your unit.

Japan is different

The one-way ticket to Japan was full of promise, until I actually arrived there and found a business with no sales, no revenues and no prospect of any sales. But there were plenty of bills to be paid. No one back in New Jersey had a clue what was happening in Japan. I began to suspect that I did not have a clue either.

Quickly I realised there were two battles to fight:

> 1 Get the business going in Japan: find some revenues, fast.
>
> 2 Manage perceptions: set expectations and sell a story to our masters in New Jersey.
>
> The story was simple: to acquire a decent business in Japan would cost at least $10 million, with all the risks of acquiring something which might not fit with our business model. We could do far better: over three years we would build a business that fitted the New Jersey business model and it would only cost $6 million, or $2 million a year.
>
> For reasons that remain obscure, they bought the story. We had just given ourselves the licence to lose (sorry, 'invest') $2 million a year in the business. We had reset expectations very low, and had sold a story which our masters liked and we could deliver.
>
> Over the next three years we racked up enough air miles to bankrupt several airlines. Managing perceptions and staying in touch takes serious effort.

The power network: career management

Management is becoming 21st century slavery, with the twist that we are all volunteering to become slaves. The hype of the 24/7 society where we can have anything, anytime and anyplace is consumer heaven. The 24/7 manager who has to do anything, anytime and anyplace lives in working hell. We wear our technology shackles with pride. Managers compete to see whose shackles are the newest and best: mobile phone, computer, internet service, blackberries and more.

Our ultimate slave drivers are the merciless demands of the market. Our immediate slave drivers are our own bosses. We have a very unequal relationship with them. They matter greatly to us, we are less important to them. If we leave in a huff, complaining about being treated like a slave, we only help make our boss look good: the boss will record that we were not up to the job, did not have the drive and were not a real contributor so they made the tough decision and let us go. They look like heroes, and we have just become zeroes.

We let ourselves become real slaves to our managers when we become totally dependent on them. If they are benign slave drivers, they will look after us and make sure we get the good jobs (not cleaning out the lavatories), get well rewarded and maybe even get promoted. If they are evil slave drivers, our lives will be a misery. Managers get to choose their bosses as often as slaves got to choose their owners.

To buy some freedom, we need to find ways of becoming less than 100 per cent dependent on the whims of our boss. We need some allies and a network of support.

Your career network: checklist

Check your career network against the following:

Sponsors

These will be at least two levels above you in the organisation. They can be critical in nudging your career in the right direction: helping you find the right positions and bosses, avoiding career traps, providing political air cover when you need to push an agenda item and giving you access to decision makers when you need it. In return, you are their eyes and ears in the organisation, and you may well provide discretionary support and effort on ideas that they are testing and programmes they are starting up. Providing you can continue to add value to them, they will help you. Senior executives often enjoy the energy and alternative perspectives provided by people who do not threaten them. You can make them into your personal coaches with great effect.

Informers

These will let you know what is going on. Particularly valuable are people who know what job opportunities and assignments are emerging. HR sometimes know this, but normally there is a grapevine which knows the informal truth long before the official truth comes out. At one bank, staff ran a book on who was going to get promoted or fired next. The odds were very accurate predictors of future events long before HR knew what was happening.

Outsiders

These can help you provide an escape route out of your organisation. Over 70 per cent of executive jobs are both found and filled by word-of-mouth

---

contacts. If you know you can move, you have a much more equal relationship with your boss. If you have nowhere else to go, you are dependent. Professionals in investment banking and in Silicon Valley can command huge salaries partly because they have great skills, but also because it is very easy in such incestuous industries for them to walk across the road to another organisation. They are not indentured slaves to their current employer.

Playing for power

There are three ways of gaining power:

1 Work for it

2 Ask for it

3 Take it

1 Work for it

Route one is to work hard, do well and hope that people recognise your contribution and offer you your dream job. This is the normal route. Sometimes you get lucky and it works. Often it does not, for the simple reason that hope is not a method and luck is not a strategy.

You need more than hope and luck. You need to be able to control your destiny: if you do not someone else will. They will not feel as passionately about your interests as you do.

If you are humble enough to rely on this route, then there are two things you can do to improve your odds of success: build a claim to fame and focus on the moments of truth.

Build a claim to fame

We all like to think we are exceptional. There are not many people who would admit to being worse than average at driving, loving, intelligence, achievement or work. At work we are surrounded by people of similar ability to ourselves. They think they are better than us, and we think we are better than them. This logical impossibility is emotionally inevitable.

We need something which easily sets ourselves apart from our colleagues. In a crowded market for promotions, you need to be able to differentiate yourself in some way. Here are three basic ways of achieving differentiation and a claim to fame:

1 *Exceptional achievement*. This has to be demonstrably better than your colleagues. In sales and trading, performance is easy to measure. In many other roles, performance is much more ambiguous.

2 *Starting something*. New initiatives are ever-present in most organisations. Not all will succeed, but they offer managers the chance to build a distinctive claim to fame, while learning and growing at the same time.

3 *Changing something*. Managers have to change things and hopefully improve them. Failure to change things ranks a manager as an administrator or caretaker. It is not enough simply to do the job: you have to show improvement.

Once you have a claim to fame, you need to stake your claim. If you do not, you will find plenty of people who come out of the woodwork to claim their share of the success you have created. There are simple ways of staking your claim to fame:

▶ Congratulate and thank people for their contribution. People like public recognition, and you are giving it to them. By congratulating them, you are also showing that you were in the lead role.

▶ Review and discuss the challenges and lessons learned. This requires a level of knowledge about the initiative which probably only you have. It demonstrates your mastery of the programme.

▶ Stay in control and build on success. Take the lead in discussing how to take the initiative to the next stage. This will keep people off your bandwagon because it implies that more work is required (which they do not have time for) and it requires deep knowledge of what is happening, which they lack.

Focus on the moments of truth

Make the most of those limited opportunities to meet senior executives. Their limited direct contact with you will influence their thinking more than all the formal HR assessments, which are often exercises in box ticking and propaganda. Moments of truth come in three broad flavours:

1   *Planned moments of truth.* These are meetings or presentations where you know you will be in front of senior executives. Take a disproportionate amount of time preparing for this event. Get coaching on their style of working and how your style will or will not work with them. Make sure any supporting material is 100 per cent professional and 100 per cent error free.

2   *Unplanned moments of truth.* These happen when you bump into a senior executive or you are unexpectedly summoned by a senior executive. Even here, some planning is possible. A good discipline is to think through why your work is relevant and useful two or three levels higher in the organisation. If you know this, you will be able to choose your priorities well, identify problems early and be ready for the unexpected encounter: you will communicate what is relevant to them. The survivalist guide to the totally unexpected event has three principles:

(a) Be positive: find solutions where others find problems. Senior executives prefer solutions to problems, but most people bring them problems.

(b) Be proactive: drive to action, which is what management is meant to be about.

(c) Be professional: honesty, clarity, focus are simple disciplines in short supply. Defensiveness, shifting blame and obfuscation are natural short-term survival strategies which do not make a good impression.

These skills are examined in more depth in Saying no to your boss (section 4.6) and Handling conflict (section 3.5).

3   *Created moments of truth.* These happen when you create the unexpected meeting with a person you need to influence. These opportunities happen regularly: before and after meetings or conferences which you know they will attend; at their regular lunchtimes, at the gym or at any other point in their daily routine. Use these opportunities the same way that you would use the unplanned moment of truth, with the one exception: give the target the feeling that they are in control of the encounter. If they believe they are in control, they will be more relaxed

and more open than if you hustle them as soon as you open your mouth. Degrading as it feels, a little flattery mixed with social talk will go far and fast in setting them at their ease.

The promotions commission: reality versus reason

We faced a mountain of promotion recommendations. There were over 50 promotion packs of about 40 pages each. We knew that they were as accurate as Pravda in the Soviet era. Each promotion package was a eulogy of unstinting praise. We needed some way of making a decision: 30 promotions were available so there were going to be more than 20 very disappointed people.

We did our best to read the truth behind the propaganda, but inevitably we always came back to two questions:

1   What has this person really achieved? Every candidate ticked all the boxes in terms of qualifications, team work, intellect, leadership and more. But only a few had a real claim to fame which we could recognise. They were easy decisions to make.

2   Who knows this person? Often they would be known from a fairly short interaction. Perhaps they had made a presentation or volunteered to do something. If that was a positive event, then the eulogy on paper became more credible. If it was a negative event, we started reading the eulogy much more critically.

In an organisation where everyone appears outstanding, this was the only way we could find of sorting the highest potential from the high potential. We probably got it wrong in some cases, at great human cost. Promotion went to the high PQ managers who had found a claim to fame, staked their claim and taken care to make sure they made a very good impression in even the shortest of contacts with members of the promotions commission.

---

2 Ask for it

Route two is to ask for the job. This is very simple and much underused.

Asking your boss for his or her job is, perhaps, inadvisable. But most careers do not go in straight lines. Unlike the pawn steadily advancing up the chess board in search of promotion, most careers make knight's moves: two steps to the side and one forwards (or even backwards) in search of a better position. Occasionally, the knight may move two steps forwards, or even two steps backwards, in search of the ideal position.

The first task of the career knight is to know where the best positions exist. In all organisations there are many different opportunities opening up all the time. If you do not know what those openings are, you cannot expect to fill them. Do not wait for HR to advertise them on the internal bulletin board. If you have built an adequate network across the organisation, you will know which initiatives and openings are emerging long before they become official.

When you know what the openings are, you have two strategies to follow:

1 Assume the cloak of invisibility.
2 Start volunteering.

If there is an undesirable opening, make sure you are very, very busy. Make sure you are indispensable on your current assignment, at least for the time being. If you are not already 100 per cent committed in terms of workload, start volunteering to do other stuff on other projects. The goal is first of all to be invisible to the assignment process, and then to be so unavailable that they cannot second you onto the death star assignment you wish to avoid.

If there is an opening which looks interesting, express enthusiasm. Ask HR and your future potential boss what they are looking for in terms of the person they need: discuss actively with them how well you fit. They may quietly be delighted to have a potential solution to their staffing problem. Reinforce your interest by providing a little work for free to help them: you can help with a proposal or a briefing. By doing this, you become the natural expert to fill the vacant role, and you build support from the boss you want to work for.

The Thai tapioca test

I was coming towards the end of an assignment. Cautiously, I found out what other assignments were in the pipeline. To my horror I found that Daniel, who liked to eat analysts for breakfast, had sold a project to do competitive analysis on the Thai tapioca market. I was not too keen on thinly disguised industrial espionage in a language I could not speak and in an industry I did not know. And I hate tapioca. I saw a nightmare looming.

➤

> I also found out that there was a Saudi marketing project. Saudi Arabia is not everyone's cup of tea and they were not going to staff it easily. But the project manager was great. So I quickly discovered unbounded enthusiasm for all things Saudi Arabian. I took the strain off the project manager by helping draft the final proposal. Meanwhile I was mysteriously busy whenever a Thai tapioca planning session was called: my cat would die (again), or I would suddenly have an urgent meeting with my existing client. I told the Saudi project manager I wanted to work with him. He was delighted to have any sort of solution to his staffing challenge, even me.
>
> Mysteriously, I dodged the bullet and found myself on the Saudi project, not the Thai tapioca project. Subsequent events led me to hope fervently that the Thai project was at least as bad as I had feared, but that is another story. . .

3 Take it

Route three is to take the job. This is highly effective and much easier than it sounds. There are two simple methods of taking the job:

- ▶ the power of the pen
- ▶ the Nike strategy: 'Just do it'.

The power of the pen

In the early stages of any project, managers tend to be using their discretionary time and effort to develop the idea. This is a pain in the backside. We all have enough to do without spending extra time on another initiative which will cause even more work. Managers may get together to shape, discuss and promote the idea but no one really wants to do the heavy lifting of making it happen. This leaves a vacuum waiting to be filled. If this is a project, assignment or programme which you like then fill the vacuum.

The easiest way to fill the vacuum is with a pen. In the meeting where the idea is being discussed, you can offer to be the scribe and work the flip chart. Everyone else will be relieved to avoided that extra little task. You are now in control of the agenda. You can shape the minutes of the meeting. There will, naturally, be things you need to follow up on as a result of the meeting to clarify. Suddenly, you are in the driving seat. You are doing the job. This takes effort to drive it forward, so you have to pick your opportunities. Because it takes effort, others are avoiding the challenge. Once you are doing the job, you will be the natural person to continue driving the programme when it gets formal approval.

A subtle variation of the power of the pen play is the administrative coup. There are always tedious administrative duties to be attended to, some of which are critical. Anything to do with governance, budgets or staffing has the potential for an administrative coup. The coup is simple to execute: offer to take over the administrative burden of this core activity. In the rush to do everything else, your offer may well be welcome. Having taken over this duty, you are now well placed to shape things the way you want them to be shaped.

The administrative coup

The start up was a real challenge. There was too much to do and not enough people to do it: finding sponsors, getting government approvals, creating the marketing programme, setting up the training, negotiating with vendors, recruiting staff.

Fortunately, a senior business person offered to sort out the administrative stuff around governance, which meant working with lawyers and the charity commission. This sounded great so we let him get on with it.

Several years later, he still had a stranglehold over governance. He had used a tedious administrative task to insert himself as chairman and his friends and colleagues as trustees. It was unclear what, if anything, they were actually contributing. We found out too late that the working with lawyers was a trivial task with lasting consequences.

The Nike Strategy: 'Just Do It'

For many years, Nike used 'Just Do It' as their advertising slogan. It could, equally, be the whole philosophy of management. We can analyse management until the stars fall from the skies, but ultimately successful managers just do it. But it takes more than wearing a Nike T-shirt to be a great athlete and it takes more than 'just do it' to land the dream job.

An aspiring manager needs to do more than act the part: he or she needs to sound and look like the real thing as well. As with Nike, style counts as much as substance. This is not a recommendation to wear Nike baseball hats in the office. It is a recommendation to follow the style fashion of the group you aspire to, to learn its language and conventions of behaviour. The more you seem like one of them, the more likely you are to become one of them. The sad reality is that management talk diversity, but value intimacy. Managers prefer people who act and think like themselves: diversity of race, sex and religion has just about become acceptable, provided that each individual can adapt to the uniform culture of the organisation. Many organisations state this explicitly: McKinsey celebrates the 'One Firm Firm'. Accenture staff were (in their Andersen Consulting days) known as Androids who had been cloned learning method one at their Chicago campus. Reputedly, there was no method two or style two in the cloning factory.

Conformity is not only about conforming to the organisation's culture. It requires discovering and conforming to the tribal rituals and standards of the group within the organisation you want to join. This can lead to some awkward choices:

- ▶ The creative group: outsized glasses and outsized opinions together with snorting copious amounts of what looked like sugar seemed to be obligatory.

- ▶ The partnership: personal tailor, with a trophy house and a trophy spouse each.

- ▶ The major financial firm: 'Put your liver on the line.' You could not afford to bottle out.

- ▶ The brokerage: suprisingly low golf handicaps for people who are meant to work so hard.

- ▶ Real estate agency: flexible ethical standards – make that sale, what-ever.

- ▶ Government agency: wait your turn, take no risk, follow procedures even if they are insane.

Just do it: the ultimate power play

He was an associate on a consulting project. The project he had been work-ing on called for a new organisation to be created. And he decided he wanted to be CEO. He had not run anything more than a bath in the past. Given the project was surrounded by senior business people, each with decades of experience, it was not clear how he was going to become CEO.

The good news about important and busy people is that they are very busy being important. They do not have spare time. So the associate started just doing it. He put together all the papers and plans required to start the new organisation. And then he started signing all his emails 'Acting CEO'. All the busy and important people were delighted: someone was taking control, making it happen and removing all the hassle.

After a while, he dropped the word 'Acting' from 'Acting CEO'. Five years later, he remains a very successful CEO.

4.3 Building power networks: becoming irreplaceable

Managers make things happen through other people. In the 19th century the mill owner could tell people what to do. In the 21st century, command and control is increasingly rare. Jobs are more specialised and matrix organ-isations are more complicated: the only way managers can make anything happen is by persuading other people to help and support them. As firms focus more on their core competencies, they also become more specialised. Managers may need to negotiate for support from outside the organisation as well as within it.

Getting decisions made and making things happen is like a giant act of cho-reography, where the manager is trying to make the organisation dance to his or her own tune. This is a challenge because many other managers either do not want to dance at all, or they want to dance to a different tune. In section 4.1 we saw the seven major sources of power. Two tasks remain:

1 Decide what role each of the dancers should play.

2 Encourage them to dance.

Roles within your network

Building a coalition for action is like a living video game: you have to work through several layers of the game acquiring the right resources and power at each level while fighting off the forces of evil that wish to derail your project, programme or initiative. In this video game, there are a series of power characters who you need to find and get on your side. If you fail to find them they are likely to emerge from the shadows as an enemy intent on your destruction: game over.

The seven key characters in the grand coalition are:

1   The player
2   The godfather
3   Users
4   Gatekeepers
5   Technocrats
6   Soldiers
7   Coaches

As you build your coalition, ask why each person wants to join the coalition. The key questions go straight back to greed, fear, idleness and risk:

▶ Greed: what's in it for them?
- ▷ accelerate their agenda, business needs
- ▷ personal paybacks around training, experience, recognition
- ▷ help them meet their targets.

▶ Fear: what is the downside for them of not helping?
- ▷ miss the bandwagon, seen in a poor light
- ▷ get sidelined, lose influence over something which might affect them
- ▷ miss targets.

▶ Idleness: how can we make it easy for them to support us?
- ▷ focus your requests on their area of expertise and interest
- ▷ create a simple first step: the 'in principle' support
- ▷ build their commitment and involvement incrementally.

▶ Risk: how can I remove fear of failure and show it will succeed?

   ▷ show some early wins, build momentum

   ▷ incremental commitments: pilot and test ideas, stage investments

   ▷ demonstrate political support: create the bandwagon effect.

As you review the list of players, you should be able to profile each player against the greed, fear, idleness and risk checklist. Marry that to their contact details and a record of when you have met them and will meet them again, and you have a comprehensive and simple guide to building your coalition for action. Each time you meet a coalition member, update your log book and note down the next steps you want and need to pursue with them.

1 The player

This is you. Your job is to build the coalition in support of your programme. Your first job is to find the godfather.

2 The godfather

The godfather, as in the film, is the person who pulls the strings and has the ultimate power. In an organisation, he or she is often referred to as the authoriser or economic buyer because they have both budget and authority. The role of the godfather is:

▶ Call the project into being.

▶ Give it support: budget, political backing as necessary.

▶ Approve and close it at the end.

Typically, the godfather is senior and has many other things to worry about so will only occasionally be involved. The godfather wants people who bring solutions, not problems. Godfathers are powerful allies and dangerous enemies. Matching the challenge to the godfather is essential: starting a project for a minor don who lacks the muscle to see the project through is an invitation to stress and disappointment. You will be struggling for support. It is also essential to meet the godfather and understand what he or she really wants. Do not rely on your boss or other intermediaries to have relayed the godfather's wishes accurately: they may simply be poor at communication or they may be adding their own agenda onto the godfather's.

3 Users

Finding users is a real challenge in this game. There are plenty of people who will claim to represent the user. User's representatives are shadows of the real thing and you score no points in dealing with them. You need the real users. The real users are the people who will be most directly affected by the outcome of your project or initiative. Only by working with real users will you understand their needs, how they work and what the real barriers are to implementing your project. They are the people who will most clearly express the need for your project: if they are not shouting for it, you may have a weak project.

IT projects are dogged by the user–provider problem. The user (the insurance underwriter, for instance) has a completely different world view from the provider (the systems developer). Each does not even understand the other's language. If you can bridge this divide, you will earn the loyalty and support of both sides.

4 Gatekeepers

These people hold the door to power. Secretaries are obvious. Giving them chocolate and flowers is obvious bribery and it is condescending. Treat them as experienced professionals in their own right, show an interest in them as people and not as mere appendages to a boss and they are likely to respond positively.

There are also some very dangerous gatekeepers. The gatekeeper from the dark side is a middling to senior manager who promises to get you access to very senior management. This sounds wonderful. But as soon as you rely on them to deliver, you will find two things happen:

1   The gatekeeper starts to make demands of you and your project. The implicit deal is that if you do not deliver some outrageous demand to them, they will block access.

2   The gatekeeper never delivers access anyway, because they are either unable or unwilling to do so.

These people hate it when you go round them. Go round them anyway: you cannot afford to be enslaved by them. It is normally possible to arrange an accidental encounter with your target executive in which your project just happens to be mentioned. You can then go back to the gatekeeper and thank them for their efforts and explain apologetically how the accidental meeting just happened and how you now have a series of meetings set up with the senior executive so the gatekeeper's services are no longer needed. Goodbye.

5 Soldiers

These are the resources with the varied skills you need to deliver the project. They may not be under your direct command. The more effort you need from each soldier, the more investment is required to recruit them.

▶ If you need the soldier for some advice or attending a meeting or two, you can normally get them to volunteer their time. Public praise of their contribution helps, and be prepared to return the compliment when they need to call on your skills as a soldier for their project.

▶ For more extensive commitments, you need to get the soldiers assigned to you. The simple rule is to refuse anyone who is offered to you. You will be offered the weakest people who no one else wants. You will be offered a combination of the untried and unknown, together with the tried, tested and failed. Projects staffed with B players struggle to achieve even a B grade: there is no one to pull them up except yourself. The only way to achieve an A grade is to get A grade soldiers, who will by definition be busy working elsewhere. A good indication of the priority of the assignment and the power of the godfather is the strength of the team you can assemble. If it is a weak team, you may have a low priority assignment and a weak godfather: this is an extreme danger sign and it is worth walking away, if at all possible. Do not let yourself be set up to fail.

6 Technocrats

Technocrats normally have permissive power (see section 4.1). They can pop out of the shadows and stop you because you have not jumped the hurdle that they want all players to jump. The key technocrats are often in finance: they check your budget numbers and business case. Seek them out early, make them into allies. Understand what they need from you to make their life easy, and they will probably respond positively. Other lurking technocrats can be found in legal, HR, health and safety, the brand 'police'. Some players treat technocrats as the enemy to be defeated: this is painful and rarely works well. Much better is to treat them as allies: invest time and effort in getting to know them and work with them. Give them some small wins in shaping your project. Lavishly praise their (minor) contributions in public. They are not used to praise and flattery. They will enjoy the limelight. As allies they can make life relatively easy for you: they will focus their venom on less cooperative players in other games.

Of technocrats, taxi drivers, babies and God

Never argue with babies, taxi drivers or God: even if you are right, it will do you no good. To this list we might add the whole army of technocrats who can, if necessary, prove that night is day and that the sea is dry. Lawyers, accountants, actuaries and IT professionals live on planets where even the boldest astronauts fear to tread. As managers, we have to deal with these alien species on a regular basis.

The essential truth is never work against the technocrats: always find a way of getting them on your side from the start.

We had been asked to value a financial group which included a bank and an insurance company. The previous consultants had been thrown out by the army of accountants and actuaries who had torn some very impressive analysis to shreds. It was hard to see how we could do any better, other than avoiding having our blood splattered over the board room like the last lot. One hint seemed to be that they really disliked being told that their share price was overvalued by about $1 billion. They wanted a much higher valuation, which we suspected was unjustifiable.

So we decided not to start any analysis at all. We just talked to the technocrats about how they saw things, about how they presented and analysed data, how they liked to do things. Slowly we started to get them to identify some of the key data and to work the data up. We had a simple system: if they produced good data and analysis (which matched our own private work) we praised it greatly. This always led to more questions, comment and analysis. If they produced any suspect work, we ignored it.

> After about a month they had arrived at a new valuation which they believed in 100 per cent, because they felt they had produced it. They now proudly announced to the board that their share price was overvalued by about $3 billion. We escaped with our blood unspilled and with the promise of more work to come.

7 Coaches

Sometimes, it is hard to believe that there are senior people in an organisation who are full of skill and goodwill: they will do things because they believe they are right and will help both the organisation and you personally. These people are like gold dust: find them and befriend them. The best coaches will have enough experience and access to understand how the politics are being played, how to deal with different individuals and how to promote your agenda. They can be your eyes and ears: they will hear and see things which you will not. Like the jilted spouse, the project manager is the last person to discover the truth about the situation. A good coach will help spot the problem even before it happens.

4.4 Using power: setting your agenda

For some people power is an end in its own right. They strive for the status and money that power brings. These are the people who mistake position for performance and status for achievement. Management should not be about position and status: it should be about performance and achievement. At the risk of repetition, the task of management is to make things happen through other people.

Once upon a time, the task of management was simpler. In a command and control organisation, the job of management was to communicate and implement the decisions of the owners and leaders of their organisation. Managers did what they were told to do. This is still the paradigm in some more traditional bureaucracies: the discretion, autonomy and power of managers is relatively limited in such organisations.

For most managers, management has become both more demanding and more rewarding. Managers can no longer afford to wait and be told what to do. Being passive and reactive is good for short-term survival because you take no risk. But taking no risk and having no initiative is not just risky in the long term: it is career suicide. Managers cannot be passive: they have to start creating and promoting agendas based on their own knowledge of what will best help the organisation move forward.

A manager's most valuable resource is time. We cannot make more of it. We are all heading towards our sell by date. Technology makes us work faster, but does not help us focus on the right things. Technology makes us more efficient (sometimes) but it does not make us more effective. We can only become more effective by focusing our limited time on the right tasks. To make the most of our time, we have to set the right agenda.

In reality, managers have to spend most of their time on maintenance activities: budgets, staffing, operational matters. Unless this is well delegated, it can absorb every hour of the day (see section 3.4 on delegation). Managers have to work on the right agenda. The right agenda has to be 'right' personally and professionally.

Personal tests of the right agenda

The first test of a good agenda is very simple and very personal. Ask yourself one question: 'How will I remember this year in five or ten years' time?' Here are some things you will not remember it for:

- the number of emails you sent
- the hours you spent in meetings
- meeting or beating budget by a percentage point or two
- details of your appraisal
- your annual bonus (unless it was exceptional, either way).

If you have a year you remember for nothing, you have just lost a year of your life. You do not have to change the world, but it helps to have something in your business life which you can remember. In a personal career which has been more of a verb ('to career through life') than a noun ('to have a sensible career'), a few professional highlights included:

- becoming the best nappy salesman in Birmingham
- putting the blue speckle in Daz
- attending business school
- working in Saudi Arabia
- leading a business in Japan
- starting a bank
- starting Teach First.

These were the times I was living life with the record button on, and everything happened in technicolor. Then there are the years I cannot remember. Life lived in shades of grey and instantly forgettable. What happened in 1998? Life with the delete button on. I got one year closer to death, and nothing else. Life should be lived with the record button on.

Two more simple personal tests of the right agenda are:

- What will I learn from this year?
- Am I simply cruising, or am I learning new skills from new experiences which will help me in the future?

Professional tests of the right agenda

This is a fundamental survival test for management. If you work on the wrong agenda for the wrong people and with the wrong people, at very best you will survive and be irrelevant. If you work on the right agenda for the right people and with the right people, you will not only survive: you will have a chance to succeed. There is no point in working 100 per cent of your time on 100 per cent the wrong agenda. Invest time and effort in making sure you are working on the right agenda.

Professionally, the right agenda requires asking two basic questions:

1   How important is this agenda to the organisation?
2   How likely are we to succeed?

The questions may be obvious, but the answers are not. It is worth drilling down to test each question more fully. If you find positive answers to each of these questions, you are probably working on the right agenda and you are likely to succeed. If not, you may want to take stock.

1 How important is this agenda to the organisation?

The importance question can be resolved by asking three more detailed questions:

1   *Visibility and relevance.* The problem or opportunity you are working on should have visibility and relevance well beyond your own department. Even if you do great things within your department, you will be seen as doing no more than your job requirement, albeit to a high standard. To make an impact, you need to work on an agenda which involves other departments horizontally and has visibility at least one or two levels up the organisation.

2   *Business impact.* This is closely related to the relevance which the problem has to senior management. It should, normally, be possible to quantify the business impact. The obvious measures are financial (costs, revenues, profit contribution). In the right circumstances, non-financial measures can also be valid (improved customer or staff retention; fewer defects, rework, complaints; faster time to market). Many of these non-financial measures have financial impact which is worth estimating and validating with finance and the relevant departments.

3   *Urgency.* Managers have much to worry about. We should probably worry about pensions, global warming and the fate of humanity. These are pretty important. In your organisation there are also probably some pretty important issues, which are quietly being ignored. In practice, managers get recognition for dealing with urgent matters with immediate impact. Putting out the fire has more value than redesigning the kitchen and dealing with today's business challenge has more value than dealing with tomorrow's challenge. This may be short term, but there is no long term unless we survive the short term. The long term is the product of a series of short terms.

If something has visibility, relevance, business impact and urgency you are likely to find that people are already starting to work on the issue and are probably getting frustrated by the challenge. If they are not working on it, ask whether the issue is really as important and as urgent as people make out.

2 How likely are we to succeed?

Most battles are won and lost before the first shot is fired. The same is true of most business battles. Make sure you are set up for success before you embark on a new challenge. It is far better to spend one month playing hard ball over the set up of a project than to spend another 12 months of misery trying to deliver an outcome which was impossible from the outset. The high PQ manager will instinctively invest very heavily in setting up an agenda for success; the naïve manager will accept a challenge out of duty and commitment. A year later, the high PQ manager will be seen to be a success, and the diligent but naïve manager will be seen to be a failure.

Failures are normally the fault of one of the four horsemen of the apocalypse of change. Avoid the four horsemen, and you are on the way to success. The four horsemen are:

(a) the wrong problem

(b) the wrong godfather

(c) the wrong team

(d) the wrong process.

(a) The wrong problem

The best answer to the wrong problem is worthless. Make sure you are working on the right problem by answering the three questions outlined in the section above about visibility and relevance, business impact and urgency.

As a manager, you have to challenge the received wisdom about the nature of the problem. Problem analysis is dealt with in section 2.4. The biggest mistake is dealing with symptoms, not root causes. Symptom management yields short-term gains which may look good but achieve nothing. For instance, cost cutting and taking tough decisions to stop spending and lay people off looks like brave and effective management. It can also be useless and destructive management if the underlying problems of lack of revenues (wrong products, wrong channels) or excess costs (poor processes, sourcing, design) are not resolved first.

(b) The wrong godfather

A good test of whether you have the right problem is whether you are able to find the right godfather for it. If it is a genuinely important, visible, high impact and urgent problem then it will be relevant and visible to a senior person who will want to sponsor you and your agenda. If no power baron wants to be your sponsor, then it is either unimportant or such toxic waste politically that it is not worth touching.

The godfather makes a critical difference at two points:

1   At start up the godfather can ensure you get the right resource, budget, team, time and support to succeed.

2   When things start getting tough, a quiet word from the godfather can remove blockages which would otherwise be insurmountable.

From a manager's perspective, a good godfather will have four main qualities:

1   Political power: they can fix things and make things happen.

2   Credibility: they will have a track record of making things happen. This gives confidence to the team and all the stakeholders and other power barons who may need to be involved. A quick chat round the coffee machine is enough to establish which senior executives have credibility and which do not.

3   Personal stake in the game: your project needs to be important to them. Altruism is not enough when the going gets tough. If they cannot walk away, they will support you well.

4   Trustworthiness. Again, the coffee machine test will establish who can and cannot be trusted. You want to know that they will be equally generous in sharing the fruits of success and failure, sharing praise and blame. You do not want to spend your whole time minding your back and minding the competing messages which you and an untrustworthy boss are circulating.

(c) The wrong team

The first test of the good godfather is whether they can help secure the right support for you to deliver on your goal. A poor team will make mountains out of molehills; a good team will make molehills out of mountains. From the manager's perspective this is the difference between failure and success and heaven and hell. Always hold out for the A team who, by definition, will already be busy elsewhere.

The right team in the context of change has three qualities:

1 Collectively they have or can access the skills to meet the challenge.

2 Members are able to work together as a team.

3 Individually they have interest and enthusiasm for the challenge.

Most managers focus on the skill question, because that is logical and safe. The team-working element is the responsibility of the manager. A good team may well have diverse styles: this is hard work and high maintenance but can be highly productive.

Perhaps the most important question is not about skill, but about will. It is not enough to do the political deal and have people assigned to you. You need to sell your project to your team members as well: they have to see relevance and value to themselves in your mission and in their role in your mission (see section 3.1 on motivation). Highly motivated people will rise to the challenge; those with low motivation will sink to the lowest level of performance to avoid performance sanctions.

(d) The wrong process

This is the least dangerous of the four horsemen of the apocalypse. If you have the right problem, the right godfather and the right team then even if you start out with the wrong process, you will have the will and skill to change course as necessary.

4.5 The art of unreasonable management: ruthlessness

Perhaps, in a perfect world, managers would always be reasonable. We do not live in a perfect world and managers are not always reasonable. The best managers are selectively unreasonable and ruthless. The worst managers are always unreasonable and ruthless. Being ruthless is not the same as being a bully, showing aggression, personalising issues and making life a misery for everyone. There are plenty of people out there who are like that. They are collecting enemies who will be only too pleased to see them fail and to help them fail when the time comes.

The art of unreasonable management has three elements:

1   when to be unreasonable and ruthless

2   how to be unreasonable and ruthless

3   how to deal with the ruthless boss.

1 When to be unreasonable and ruthless

Sun Tsu's three rules of warfare make a useful reappearance at this stage. Only fight (be unreasonable and ruthless) when there is:

▶ a prize worth fighting for

▶ certainty of success

▶ no other way of winning the prize.

The times it is worth being ruthless are when the stakes are highest. This means:

▶ budget negotiations

▶ target setting

▶ team formation

▶ assignments and promotions.

To make this simple: if you work on the right assignment with a great team and a good budget to meet sensible targets, you have won 80 per cent of the battle. If you are on the wrong assignment with a lousy team, a thin budget and absurd targets, start looking for another job. There may be other battles you need to fight, but do not waste personal time and equity on fighting skirmishes: even if you win the skirmish you will lose a friend, and you could pay for that dearly when the big battles start. If you see a skirmish, make your position clear and then concede, preferably by negotiating for something in return for your concession.

2 How to be unreasonable and ruthless

Great things are rarely achieved by reasonable people. Look at the heroes of history and you will not find many reasonable people among them: from Charlemagne to Churchill, Genghis Khan to Kennedy you find events shaped by people who achieved the impossible. The great entrepreneurs from Getty to Gates are not modest people who settled for a reasonable outcome: they played to win and to win big. Within your own organisation, you can probably identify people who achieve much: they may well be among the more ruthless and unreasonable managers in the organisation. Meanwhile, many reasonable and decent managers find themselves sidelined.

It is possible to be ruthless without being unpleasant. The key is to understand that you can be unreasonable and ruthless about the outcomes, while still being reasonable about the method of getting there. The following are good illustrations.

Budget negotiations

▶ Be very clear about the acceptable goals and why they are acceptable. Then stick limpet-like to that position. If you concede anything, negotiate for something in return. Be very clear about the consequences and risks of any change. Make any deviance from your position feel very risky.

▶ Set expectations early: anchor the discussion at the right level before the formal budget round starts (see section 2.6).

▶ Use both the formal and informal processes to make your stand. Do not rely on the formal staff process to deliver the outcome you want: lobby hard with key decision makers behind the scenes. Make sure you have a story to sell them: the decision makers are going to back you, a story, the numbers and their staff in roughly that order of priority. If you have credibility and a good story, you should be able to sell the outcome you need.

Target setting

This is the mirror image of budget negotiations, and the same principles apply. Always set one against the other: a change in budget should be mirrored by a change in targets.

If you are setting the targets for your team, the same rules apply but with the intent of achieving the opposite outcome: to set the most stretching goals possible without actually breaking the team.

Team formation

▶ Always hold out for the A-team. Typically, new assignments are staffed with the untried and untested, together with a few who have been tested and found wanting.

▶ Go round the formal assignment process. Sell your assignment to individuals you want on your team. Build their enthusiasm, help them identify a way out of their current responsibilities. Spot the good people who are frustrated by their current managers and cultivate them, even if you do not need them right away. When you do need them, it will be much easier if you already have a good relationship with them and they trust you.

▶ Move people on. This does not have to be unpleasant. Do not focus on why someone messed up. Focus on what they can do well, and where their talents are best used (elsewhere). Keep looking around the organisation to see if there is a slot which they could fill (where you can dump the person). Focusing on the positives is good for the individual but also means that you can move them on faster and with less conflict than if you focus on the negatives.

Assignments and promotions

▶ Work the networks. Find out where and when the interesting assignments are emerging. In many cases, these early stage initiatives have minimal budget and depend on voluntary effort to scope them. Volunteer your time. Scope the initiative to suit your needs. If you like the outcome, you will be in a prime position to have the role in the initiative which you designed for yourself. Let your future potential boss know how excited you will be working for them. Equally, make yourself highly unavailable and over-committed on essential work if there is a nightmare assignment coming up.

▶ Find a sponsor. A quick way to the top is to hang onto the coat tails of a high-flying executive: they all need a team they can trust and depend on. If you are smart, have more than one sponsor so that you are not left high and dry if your main sponsor blows up or leaves the organisation. Volunteering to do interesting odd jobs in your spare time is a quick way to get noticed and appreciated by senior executives.

▶ Set career expectations with your boss at an early stage, and then keep on reinforcing your claim. The essential discussion is called 'What do I have to do to get promoted?' Bosses hate being cornered this way, but the conversation helps by:

  ▷ clarifying what may be ambiguous

  ▷ forcing the boss to take your career prospects seriously

  ▷ making it difficult for the boss to avoid putting you up for promotion when the time is right.

How to deal with the ruthless boss

Ruthless bosses are not necessarily good or bad. They can be good for the business and bad interpersonally or vice versa, or any good/bad combination you care to create. Whatever your personal reaction to such a person, do not judge them on personal impact. Evaluate them carefully from a power perspective: will they help or harm your position and prospects in your organisation?

It pays to separate out style and substance in a ruthless boss. You will normally find this leads to one of two types of ruthlessness:

Effectively ruthless for the organisation	Painfully ruthless for self
Fights selectively: big battles	Fights on everything
Inflexible about outcomes, flexible on means	Inflexible on ends and means: 'My way or no way'
Focus on business imperatives	Personalises issues and challenges
Future focus, create win/wins	Blame culture, win/lose
Stretches people: climate of opportunity	Breaks people: climate of fear
Total commitment given and returned	Total commitment expected but not returned
Total persistence in chasing a goal: high trust	Chops and changes to suit personal needs.
Ambitious for organisation and oneself	Ambitious for oneself

If you are managed by a painfully ruthless boss, you have a problem: you will be experiencing considerable pain. You have a series of choices to make.

If the ruthless boss is a winner and trustworthy, you may want to align yourself with the devil. This may mean selling your soul, but a successfully ruthless boss needs loyal lieutenants. You will be able to rise fast through the organisation on the coat tails of the devil, if you can accept the loss of your soul.

If the boss is a winner but not trustworthy, be very careful. The devil will demand total loyalty, but will not return it. Some simple survival mechanisms for living with such a boss include:

▶ *Loyalty*. Disloyalty is the greatest cardinal sin for all managers. It breaks the bond of trust. Loyalty means always backing the boss, even on unpopular decisions. It means no bad mouthing in private: word will get back to the boss eventually, and then you are dead meat.

▶ *Flattery*. Devils have huge egos which need constant massaging. Convince the devils that you are a loyal follower and want to learn their dark secrets. They may look after you well, until they decide to dump you.

▶ *Do not take it personally*. However offensive the devil is personally, do not take it that way. Focus on solutions, actions and the future personally and with the boss. Change the devil's agenda into a similar action, solution and future focus by relentless role modelling.

▶ *Sit it out.* The corporate carousel moves round fairly fast. Few bosses last more than one or two years. You can learn much from all bosses, even if all the lessons are negative.

▶ *Prepare your escape route.* Find other sponsors in the organisation, find other opportunities and go for them at the right time. Explain to your devil boss that you are simply seeking the right personal development opportunities and experience: pretend you like working for the devil boss, you simply need new experiences.

4.6 Saying 'no' to your boss: surviving insanity

Managers must be able to say 'no' to their boss if they are to have any control over their own destiny. If you cannot say 'no', then you are at the mercy of the whims and judgement of your boss. If the boss is both benign and has good judgement, you will find yourself working on the right agenda and the right problem. But this is not a risk that always pays off over a long career. Saying no is an art form that has to be learned.

Saying 'no' to your boss is harder than resisting ideas from elsewhere in the organisation. It is harder to ignore your boss than it is to ignore your colleagues. If you are close to your boss, it pays to be direct: say 'No' and explain why in terms the boss understands so that he or she realises that it is in his or her own best interests not to proceed. As you do this, be clear about the risks and consequences of proceeding, but also try to come up with an alternative. It pays to be positive, particularly with a negative message. You need to offer solutions, not just problems.

So you need to deal with the issue, and with the boss. The challenge of this game is to find ways of saying 'no' without actually saying 'no'. Risking alliterative overload, remember the three P's of saying 'no': priorities, process and people.

Priorities

The priorities argument buys time without forcing you to oppose the idea. It forces your boss to think through the consequences of starting something new (something else will have to take a back seat) and will force some uncomfortable choices about what is most important and urgent. Even if you support the idea completely, you should still have this discussion. Typically, the priorities discussion will kick off with one of two questions:

1 How does this fit with my other priorities? Which ones would you like me to put back/defer for this idea?

2 Should we do this before or after X episode (which is more urgent and/or on the critical path)?

Process

The process discussion can also be very positive. This is where you can show you are thinking about solutions, not just problems. At the same time, you are still forcing discussion about possible risks, consequences and alternatives. This is a discussion which can slowly turn a bad idea into a good one. A good process discussion will often start with:

▶ Could we do it another way instead? (better, faster, cheaper, less risky)

▶ How can we set this up for success? (people, budget, time: connects to priorities)

People

This is a discussion about fit: are you the right fit for the project? It is a discussion you do not want to have too often with a boss, who will start to doubt whether you are fit for anything. But it is often an elegant way of avoiding a direct attack on the idea and can work well if you have an alternative in mind. A neat way of doing this is to suggest that someone else take the lead, but you will find time to help, support and direct the other person as necessary. This takes you out of the firing line without being seen to be unsupportive. The questions to raise are:

▶ Who would be ideal to lead this?

▶ How best can I support this? In what role (preferably not leading it)?

4.7 Power and integrity: from morality to survival

Many people in power lose their moral compass. The great sinners are obvious: the men with moustaches who featured so much in the last world war were not a great advertisement for the virtues of power. In any organisation, you can find people who are only too happy to corrupt themselves at the first opportunity: over-claiming on expenses and achievement, getting their snouts in at the trough to feed on the gravy train of entitlement and privilege. So what has integrity got to do with power?

In terms of business power, integrity has nothing to do with morality. It is far more important than that. In business, integrity means doing what you say. This is the essence of trust and performance. If you do not do what you say, people will not trust you. If people do not trust you, they will not want to be managed by you or to work alongside you. Integrity is not about morality: it is about survival.

Integrity is at the heart of a performance culture. Sincerity may be nicer, but is useless in business. Sincere people will say: 'I will try to. . . I hope to.' People with integrity say 'I will. . .'

There is a huge gap between sincerity (trying earnestly and diligently) versus doing. Trying does not count: only doing counts. Investors are not interested that the CEO tried to hit the profit goal: the CEO either succeeded or failed. Promising to try carries the seeds of excuses for failure: 'I tried but. . . competition cut prices/a recession started/a supplier let us down/ we did not get enough support/there was too much air in the sky.'

Sincere people may be nice, but they are not effective. Integrity may not be nice, but it is effective. Integrity counts when it comes to consequence management: deliver on promises when a team member performs well and deliver when they perform poorly. Always fulfil your side of the bargain with team members if you are to retain their loyalty and respect. Once you gain respect you start to gain power.

4.8 Taking control: telling stories

A previous British Prime Minister, John Major, was attacked by one of his colleagues for 'being in office, but not in power'. Major did not survive in office much longer, either. Managers quickly learn that there is a difference between status and power. Managers are not just given control: they have to take control.

In essence, taking control is simple: know what you want to do. If you do not know what to do, you are not in control. Events are in control. You may land up somewhere good, but through none of your own efforts.

Some things you know you have to do. The whole annual cycle of budgets and performance reviews are events to which all managers must apply themselves. But these events are simply a means to an end: the objective of management is not to deliver budget papers and performance reviews. Managers have to achieve budgets and performance. This normally means that you have to do something *different* from what was happening before. Doing the same as before and expecting a better result than before is an exercise in wishful thinking.

Sometimes this is called having a vision. This conjures up images of Martin Luther King and 'I have a dream. . .' For most managers, if you have a vision like that, keep it to yourself. In management terms a vision is no more than a simple story which has three parts:

1   This is where we are going
2   This is how we are going to get there
3   This is how you can help.

Some people add an optional fourth statement 'This is where we are'. This simply helps explain the relevance and importance of 'where we are going'.

Dwelling too long on the present and the past is not a good way of driving to the future.

1 This is where we are going

Giving direction is one of the keys to management. Direction needs to be consistent and predictable. The team needs to have some way of understanding priorities and making choices without always referring back to their manager. They need to know where to focus their personal efforts. This is where it helps to have a simple story which tells the team where they should be trying to get to.

'Where we are going' will typically either be a clear goal, or a relevant theme. Goals might include:

- ▶ make budget this year
- ▶ acquire three new clients this year
- ▶ cut costs by 15 per cent
- ▶ introduce one new product
- ▶ create a new test market programme.

Themes could include ideas like:

- ▶ professionalise the way we work
- ▶ accelerate decision making
- ▶ become more customer focused
- ▶ simplify work processes and patterns.

Some managers combine a goal and a theme: the theme is the method by which they will achieve the goal. Making things this simple takes effort, insight and judgement. Once a manager has a story like this, the path to control is clear: the manager has crafted an agenda with which to drive the team and focus it. The manager controls events, rather than being controlled by events.

The Soviet pin factory

The Five Year Plan had been approved with its usual 100 per cent support. Gosplan now had to convert the plan into detail. Eventually, it got round to the target for pins. The Plan called for a 500 per cent increase in the amount of pins produced. Seeing the sense of economies of scale, Gosplan decided to focus one factory on producing 'Pins for the People'.

The factory, which had been turning out Glorious and Revolutionary tractors, was dismayed to see that it was required to produce 20 tonnes of pins a year. They were all tractor heads, and did not fancy becoming pin heads. The factory manager devised a plan to meet the goal in one week, leaving the other 51 weeks for the business of tractor making.

At the end of week one the factory had produced one giant 20 tonne pin which would be of no use to even the stoutest babushka.

At the end of week two, the factory manager was helping fulfil the Soviet salt mining goal and Gosplan was wondering if there might be more to this business of setting targets. . .

---

2 This is how we are going to get there

Saying where you want to go is the easy bit: getting there is harder. Once you have a destination in mind, you will need to show that the goal is:

- ▶ relevant to the needs of the department
- ▶ achievable.

Most important is to focus on a few easy wins. Everyone likes to feel that they are backing a winner. A one-year goal for the department is too big: find some things that the team can start working on now so it can start seeing some early progress. You do not need to lay out the whole year in advance, as long as you are clear about the end point and the starting points.

3 This is how you can help

This is where you have to convert a general story about the department into a story which is relevant to each team member. People like to feel wanted, so show that they are important and can contribute.

Review the departmental goals individually with each team member. This is a great opportunity to set expectations about what you want to achieve and how you want to work. In return, expect to hear what team members want from you in terms of their careers, opportunities, skills and working style. As with the team as a whole, identify for each team member some early wins where they can start to make a contribution and make progress. This builds confidence on both sides: if they are unable to deliver some agreed, simple and early wins, it may be time to get worried about performance and capability.

Do this well and you will have created a psychological contract with each team member where you are both committed to what each other wants. You will have taken control of both the team as a whole and each individual within it through mutually agreed goals, actions and working styles.

4.9 Managing change: people, not projects

The received wisdom is that management is all about change. Perhaps it should be. But most managers most of the time are not keen on change. It represents risk, uncertainty and even more effort than the regular day job. The only people who are addicted to change are management consultants (change means fees and they are not at risk from the consequences of their actions) and CEOs (change tells the board that they are Doing Something, and since they are in control of the change they have little to fear from it).

Because change is seen to be central to management, management naturally claims to be doing it. There are retail financial institutions and public sector institutions where they do little more than change the wall calendar once a year, but even they will talk about the ever-increasing pace of change and the challenge it represents. This perception may be wholly false. Perceptions may be imaginary, but the consequences of perceptions are real. If managers feel that they are already changing fast, then any more change will take them well outside their comfort zone. Suddenly, you will hear many clever and rational arguments about why the change is very risky and doomed to cause chaos. Rational arguments are often no more than a plea for help from threatened individuals.

Change is the land of FUD: fear, uncertainty and doubt. Managers do not like to go there. Most managers prefer safer territory: project management. They then really confuse matters by calling project management 'change management'. As we shall see, this semantic slip is dangerous.

Change, like people, is not easy to put in neat little boxes. In principle, people should not be put in any sort of box until they are dead. But behind this messy reality, there are some consistent rules of success and failure. Every movie is unique, but most follow familiar themes. The same is true of change: each change is unique and succeeds or fails in its own unique way. But there are common themes behind both the successes and failures. Learning from personal experience is painful: what follows will help you learn from the experience of others.

The most important theme is to set the change up for success, as outlined above. That means:

- the right problem
- the right godfather
- the right team
- the right process.

Here, we will focus on 'the right process' in three bite-sized chunks:

1 Managing the change journey
2 Managing resistance
3 Offering resistance.

1 Managing the change journey

There are some practical ways of helping people through this emotional roller-coaster. If they become too stressed, they will become dysfunctional. They need your help to stay productive. The key principles are:

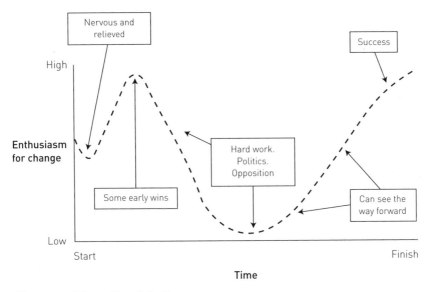

Change and the valley of death

▶ Incremental commitments. Do not ask people to do too much too soon. Stage their commitments. Start with something easy for them to do. This has two effects:

1 It builds their confidence: they perceive that they can succeed.

2 It creates a sense of obligation: having started, they will feel obliged to see the whole effort through.

▶ Stretch, but do not break people. Change, if it is serious, will take people outside their comfort zone. This can be exciting for them and lead to increased performance if they are well managed. But if they are stretched too far, they become too stressed. Like a mountaineer getting altitude sickness, they need to go all the way back to their comfort zone to recover. Then the process of staged commitments, increasing commitment and stretch can start slowly again. A common mistake is to keep forcing the pace and not give people proper recovery time. Look after the people, and they will look after the tasks. Do not let the tasks defeat the people.

▶ Focus on the positives. Recognise and reinforce the right behaviours and performance. Find something that each person is doing well, recognise it and build their confidence. Where there are problems, help the team drive to solutions and action as fast as possible: do not let them dwell on problems and on what they cannot do. Even if there is only a small thing they can do to contribute to a big problem, get them to do it.

▶ Be firm on goals, flexible on the means. Goal focus is not just about what must be achieved, but why it must be achieved. Achieving the goal will have positive consequences for the organisation and the individual: keep them focused on that prize so they see the value and relevance of what they are doing. But then allow them flexibility over how they get there: give them a sense of empowerment, control and responsibility.

▶ Set expectations early. If people expect to go through a valley of death, they do not panic when things get tough. We told one CEO to expect a valley of death experience. For the next two months he was like a child asking, 'Are we there, yet,' at each new setback. He calmly steered the organisation through the tough period because he was ready for it.

▶ Find some early wins. A few symbolic acts will often help convince people that you are serious about this change and that there is real momentum. People will start to climb aboard the bandwagon when they see it is moving.

2 Managing resistance

Most of the principles of managing resistance are covered in more detail under Influencing people (section 3.2), Building power networks (section 4.3) and Handling conflict (section 3.5). If the project has been set up the right way, most of the resistance will have been overcome before the project even starts.

But one danger lurks. Any change attracts resistance. The resistance will be most vocal from people who perceive that they have the most to lose. They will make a large amount of noise. Meanwhile the majority will keep silent. You can see the same effect when the government changes tax and spending priorities. The losers make a huge fuss, the winners keep very quiet.

The trap for the PQ manager is getting bogged down in debate with the minority. The more you listen to those in the minority, the more you

legitimise their point of view. In effect, you give them a veto over your programme. At worst they will stop it: at best they will merely delay it, weaken
it and cause huge disruption.

The best way to deal with such obstacles is to navigate around them. Focus
your efforts on enthusing the mass of people (and the critical opinion for-
mers and decision makers). As they begin to give their tacit support to your
efforts, the resistance army will start to feel isolated. As the train leaves the
station they will have a choice: get on the train, stay behind or lie on the
tracks in front of the train. No matter: the train will not stop. In business,
the resistance army will slowly break down: some will join you, some will
go into hiding and some may seek other opportunities elsewhere.

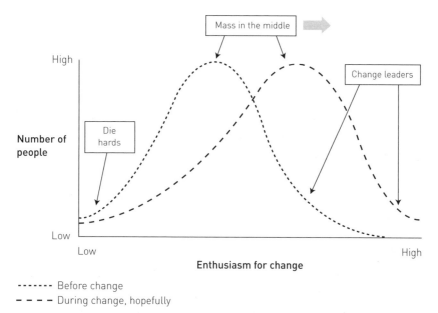

------- Before change
- - - - During change, hopefully

Shifting the change bell curve

3 Offering resistance

Occasionally, you will see a puff of insanity appear from another part of the
organisation. The insanity normally appears in the form of an initiative
which is in response to a crisis, or in response to a conference or a meeting
with consultants where they have just got hooked on the latest fad. One
way or another, the idea looks bad, smells bad and is bad. If you have a very

good relationship with the executive behind the idea, you can invite him or her for a quiet walk, explain their insanity and save them from embarrassing themselves. Often, this is not an option. You suddenly see the email traffic which is gearing the organisation to tilt courageously at a few windmills. The question is how to resist this.

Unless you are very powerful or very desperate, outright opposition to a new idea is a career-limiting move. You will make powerful enemies who will cast you as negative, unhelpful, resistant and a non-team player. This is not the ideal profile to carry into your next appraisal meeting. Fortunately, there are some successful intermediate strategies which can defeat most ideas without opposing them. In the rough order of deployment the strategies are as follows.

Do nothing

This is devastatingly effective. It leaves all the pressure on your colleagues to make something happen, to prove their case and build momentum. Indifference is hard to overcome. As soon as you start to engage in debate, even in opposition, you have recognised their agenda and they can now force a resolution in which you ultimately accept or defeat their idea. If you pursue the 'do nothing' strategy make sure you are very busy elsewhere, to show that you are not just being idle. Also, keep a close watch on what is happening: if it is clear that the agenda item is building momentum, you may need to escalate resistance.

Buy time

This is a variation of the 'do nothing' strategy. The idea is to allow enough time for the idea to blow itself up. If it is a really bad idea, other people will want to shoot it down anyway. Or they might quietly convert it into an acceptable idea. Or you may discover that in reality the idea was not as bad as you first thought. Buying time is normally done by a procedural ploy, which runs along the lines of: 'That is an interesting idea, we really should look at it more when the budget/reorganisation/IT programme is complete.' Pick an event which you know is both relevant and unhelpful to the agenda item. If you pick the right argument, you will not engage in debate about the agenda, but you will be debating when the debate should start. It is enough to drive the advocate of the insane idea insane.

Be positive

Reach out to the person with the insane idea. Show that you are willing to work with them. They are probably feeling some pressure from the resistance they are encountering elsewhere and will be delighted that someone is being positive. They will see you as an ally. Sit down with them and explore the idea more fully. Find out why they are promoting the idea. As you discuss the idea, you should find opportunities to shape it better. Ideally, you will be able to hijack the idea so that it fulfils some of your agenda needs as well.

Procter & Gamble: being positive and the art of the nice save

Some advertising agencies live down to their reputations for misapplied creativity. As clients, we loved their creativity and had to find a way of converting their latest insanity into something faintly relevant to the products we were trying to sell. The challenge was to do this without upsetting the outsized but highly fragile egos of the creative types who would flounce out of meetings at the first hint of criticism.

So we invented the idea of the 'nice save': we would always find something to be positive about. Perhaps we could only be positive about the production values. 'Production values' meant little more than the feel of the advertising, as opposed to the substance. Perhaps we might appreciate the way they bothered to feature our product, and not just their creative, alien, line-dancing hyenas. We would encourage them to feature the product even more.

By quietly building on the good things, and equally quietly trying to ignore the silly things, we would discover some advertising which would work and which we would pay for.

Do a deal

Supporting an idea takes time, effort and priority. Managers know this. So they expect to deal. You might help them with their idea, but you need some help in another area in return.

Get help

It is dangerous to ask a boss to kill an idea for you. But you can ask your sponsor or coach for advice on how to handle a situation. Explain what is happening and he or she may guide you to a smart solution. He or she may also have a quiet word in the background, and then you mysteriously find the idea has disappeared without you attacking it.

4.10 People and change: through the valley of death

Project managers often like to call themselves change managers, because it sounds much more sophisticated. They are following the same road as personnel (sorry: HR managers, human capital management, strategic talent management) and sales (woops: client relationship officers, key account managers, market executives, development associates).

Behind the harmless semantics, there is some serious confusion. Project management is largely an IQ skill which focuses on building, or sometimes, changing things like IT systems, production lines and major civil engineering works. It will typically involve the following sorts of activities:

- ▶ drawing up job specifications
- ▶ creating risk and issue logs (project managers feel strongly about the difference between a risk and an issue, but please do not ask)
- ▶ sizing the job: people, time, materials, money
- ▶ defining the critical path and what tasks need to happen in which order: put the foundations in before building the roof; open the door before trying to walk through it
- ▶ measuring and monitoring progress
- ▶ creating project plans with all the symbols which show decision points and pathways that most of us struggle to understand.

These are highly valuable disciplines which are essential when managing complex tasks.

At the end of a well-managed project, things will have changed. But people will not have changed simply as a result of building a new factory or IT system. To make a project truly succeed, you have to change what and how people do things as well. This is the essence of change management as opposed to project management. It returns us to the heart of the role of a manager: making things happen through other people.

Effective change management is about people, not just projects. We will explore five of the most common ways to affect people in the organisation:

1 Changing what people do: roles, responsibilities, job descriptions

2 Changing how people do things: skills

3 Changing how people and tasks are organised: processes and procedures

4 Changing how people are measured, rewarded and recognised: information, measurement, appraisal and incentive systems

5 Changing how people behave: cultural change in its widest sense.

The high IQ skills of project management do not help a manager faced with the deep EQ and PQ requirements of change management: changing people. Unlike buildings or IT systems, people have minds of their own with their own hopes and fears. They will argue back, avoid and evade, cause trouble, act emotionally and politically. They will act in their own self-interest, tempered by the interests of the organisation. Change is a messy reality that does not lend itself to being captured on neat little critical path analyses with elegant box and wire diagrams in a piece of project management software.

1 Changing what people do

Reorganising is often taken to be structural change: moving the boxes around the organisation chart to hope that something better will happen as a result. Structural change meets with increasing cynicism from managers who have seen it all before: centralisation to decentralisation and back again, organising around products, customers, functions or markets according to the fashion du jour.

There are the three sides to any reorganisation: IQ, EQ and PQ. The intellectual, rational reason for the reorganisation is the most common and least effective reason for the reorganisation. The benefits of reorganisation come from its emotional and political impact, if this is well handled:

▶ *Rational aspects of reorganising.* This is where consultants get very excited and draw up lots of charts, do job sizing and profiling and create countless job descriptions. They often create needless complexity and bureaucracy to justify themselves. The real problem with the rational approach to reorganisation is that there is very often no way of knowing, or proving, that one organisation structure is definitively better than another.

▶ *Emotional aspects of reorganising.* Reorganising at its most basic level is a call to arms for the organisation. It is a way of saying something like: 'We have to get closer to the customer, so now we are moving away from a product-focused structure to a customer-focused structure.' Change the structure and back that up with changes in measures, rewards, processes and procedures, and people will start to believe the story. At an individual level, the reorganisation is a great opportunity to reset the psychological contract with each member of the team: it is a way of saying: 'Here is a new world, now let's work out what we both have to do to succeed in that new world.' (See the box below.)

▶ *Political aspects of change.* A very good reason to reorganise is to overthrow the power barons. For example, Martha was appointed to run the European operations of a large systems house. In a highly macho culture, the power barons were determined to keep her at bay. They all had elegant reasons why their part of the organisation was unique and could not help the cost drive. So Martha reorganised the entire team (with one ritual execution of a power baron who was offered an unacceptable job and left). She knew that the new organisation was no better than the last one, with one difference: the power of the power barons had been broken. They were all in unfamiliar territory, they could not use their old excuses and they had seen what resistance led to. Martha was now very firmly in control of the macho barons.

Setting the new pyschological contract

It was a Sunday morning. We knew we had to announce the reorganisation tomorrow morning. Everything was in place: the piles of job descriptions, the PowerPoint presentations, the Q&A sheet, the organisation charts and the web pages. And it felt hollow: there was something missing. We looked

---

at all the paper and realised that what was missing were the people: they had been lost in the deluge of analysis.

We started to think about each individual and what it meant for them personally: their hopes and fears and what we needed from them to make the reorganisation become a success. Slowly, the reorganisation came to life.

For each individual we identified:

▶ what would be different for each individual

▶ how the reorganisation could help them personally

▶ their likely personal concerns and how we could help them

▶ what we needed from them in terms of changed performance, skills or style.

As the organisation rolled out, we sat down with each individual and discussed this new psychological contract: our commitments to each other. This psychological contract between each boss and his or her team members turned out to be far more powerful than the dry job descriptions which rapidly got consigned to the waste basket.

2 Changing how people do things

Raising and changing skills is a constant struggle for managers themselves and for the people they manage.

The manager's career journey is marked by a complete change in the sorts of skills he or she needs to master. Early in a career, managers need to learn their trade. These craft skills may be accounting, IT, law or marketing. For the most part, people are keen to learn such skills:

▶ They know they do not yet have mastery of their craft.

▶ They know that mastery is essential to career progression.

▶ The knowledge is well documented and can be learned with effort.

These craft skills become decreasingly important as the manager's career progresses. Someone who is still cutting code or doing stock checks for the audit is probably not a senior manager.

The skills that become far more important are people skills: getting other people to do things. A manager who cannot get other people to do things is not managing. Simple observation within your own organisation will show a few managers who can do this very well, and many more who are somewhere between adequate and abysmal.

The toughest challenge is to learn and then upgrade people skills: motivating, influencing, delegating, directing and managing conflict and different styles. But this is where training fails badly. An extraordinary number of managers find that they are busy arranging yoga lessons for their cat, or whatever their excuse may be, which means that they cannot attend your lovingly crafted people skills workshop. People skills training has precisely the wrong dynamics compared to craft skills training:

▶ Most managers do not want to admit that they have poor people skills: going on a training course is seen as a sign of weakness. And most managers like to think they are good with people.

▶ Managers do not see the relevance of the workshops to their careers: they will have far more pressing needs to meet some immediate challenges.

▶ The skills required are not well understood or well documented: we are dealing with tacit knowledge, not explicit knowledge. Into this vacuum step many charlatans and gurus who claim to have found the answer: all their answers contradict each other and it is not clear that their solution fits your problem anyway. They offer one miracle solution for all problems from drooping morale to drooping profits.

Building people skills is a huge challenge. Training courses simply do not work. When we asked managers how they had learned their way of managing and leading we gave them the following options:

▶ books

▶ courses

▶ peers

▶ bosses

▶ role models

▶ experience.

Essentially, everyone said that they had learned from peers, bosses, role models and experience. That makes sense. We see someone do something well, and we might try to copy it. We see someone blow up, and we quietly make a note not to step on that particular land mine ourselves. We beg, borrow and steal our management DNA from those around us to create our own unique management profile which works in our context. To the fury of the gurus, we find something which works in practice but not necessarily in theory.

This gives managers the clues about how they can enhance the people skills of themselves and their teams. There are three basic mechanisms:

1   Coaching. This is covered in more detail in section 3.3.

2   Peer group learning. Let people learn from each other about what really works (see the box below). The essence of this is to create a structured journey of structured observation and discovery. Tap into the collective experience of the group and identify what works in practice in the current context. Done well, this is also an opportunity to help people rethink what they do. Learning from peers has credibility and relevance which few outsiders can match, but it has to be well structured.

3   Building hinterland fast. Good managers tend to 'have hinterland'. They have a range of experiences and perspectives to draw on when faced with unfamiliar challenges. This is where outsiders can help, not by offering answers, but by offering alternative perspectives and experiences. No single experience or perspective will work for everyone: the idea is to give enough alternatives so that you allow people to learn from what they want to. At the risk of shameless self-promotion, my work with indigenous tribes in Papua New Guinea and Mongolia, in the Arctic (the Saami) and with the Tuareg (Mali and Libya) gives managers an insight into ways of surviving environments that are even tougher than most business environments. See www.territorymapping.net

---

Peer group learning in practice

Teaching experienced salespeople to sell is dangerous. Like most managers, they think they know it all. And when it comes to the arcane world of life insurance products, any trainer is right to feel fear. So we turned the confidence of the sales people on its head. We let them show off.

> First, we analysed who was best at selling different products to different customers. We developed a very basic selling model with them (see section 3.2). We then got the best salesperson in each category together in groups to share their secrets. This was their moment of glory. They all tried to outdo each other with their insight, which we duly documented.
>
> We structured their output and rolled it out in workshops which got everyone else to build on the frameworks and insights of the top salespeople. Everyone else was very keen to take part in these events: understanding how the best salespeople really worked was a recipe for increasing their own personal sales and annual bonus.
>
> At the end of the process we had a sales formula which would certainly fail in theory: it succeeded wildly in practice.

3 Changing how people and tasks are organised

Process change is very powerful and very misused. Used well, it helps an organisation improve marketplace performance in terms of quality, cost and customer experience. The essence of process change is to turn the organisation on its side. Most organisations tend to think functionally. This is human nature. We all look at the world from where we stand, be it in customer service, logistics, operations or any of the support functions. This makes it difficult to achieve two things:

- *Cost efficiency*. We can cut departmental costs, but many of our costs are driven by the demands of other departments and we cannot see what knock-on effects our cost cuts will have elsewhere. Cost cutting in the absence of process focus is a crude hacking at costs which results in political turf battles as each department tries to protect its own territory.
- *Market effectiveness*. The traditional functional view of the world encourages each department to see other departments as their customer. The real customer, who buys our services and pays our bills becomes an invisible and remote being.

Cost inefficiency and market ineffectiveness is not a recipe for success. Good process focus overturns the functional focus. By looking at a process (new product development, order fulfilment, customer service, trade execution) from end to end managers can see how their departmental actions link together. Managers rarely see how they fit into the whole business (from 'sheep to shop' in the rag trade, or from 'soup to nuts' for gastronomes). Once they can see the big picture, they can improve things by playing a managerial equivalent of a parlour game called 'Just a Minute'. In 'Just a Minute' you have to speak for a minute without repeating the same word, without hesitating and without deviating. It is fiendishly difficult to do this. The reengineering equivalent of 'Just a Minute' is to redesign a core business process so that it works without:

- hesitation: avoid any delays in the process
- deviation: avoid any unnecessary activities which add no value
- repetition: avoid rework as a result of poor quality.

The result should be a process which achieves success in the corporate Olympic games of betterfastercheaper.

To succeed, process redesign needs to start with the customer. Start by working out what the customer experience should look like, and work back from there. Do not start with what you already have: it may be broken. Incremental improvement of a broken system simply helps the bad survive longer. Starting with a blank sheet of paper based on customer needs gives you a chance of focusing the organisation successfully.

The downsides of process redesign are great. In many cases reengineering has become cost cutting with a smile, where the smile is an optional extra. It has become a dirty word. Mention reengineering, and people imagine hordes of junior consultants arriving to map your existing processes in great detail and at great expense before firing you.

Delivering successful process redesign is a corporate overhaul which includes: rethinking how to serve the customer; redesigning processes; changing the structure, rewards, measure and information systems to support the new redesign; changing skill sets; changing the way people work. It is ambitious and requires very strong political support. Few managers get to initiate a true, company-wide process redesign. If you hear that such a redesign is going to happen, it normally pays to be on the inside helping the redesign. Being on the outside your risk of being redesigned out of a job increases dramatically.

A short history of business processes

Around 1996 the West rediscovered the art of changing processes and called it process reengineering. Japan had been focused on process engineering for a long time, except they called it things like *kaizen* and TQM. They scared the West out of deep complacency, which helped everyone except for the employees of industries they decimated.

The West itself had always known of the importance of processes, but had somehow forgotten about them. Adam Smith, in his book *Wealth of Nations*, describes the extraordinary productivity and quality gains that could be achieved through process management in pin making. A single artisan pin maker executing the whole process was slow and inefficient. A group of unskilled workers, each of whom performed one small step in the pin making process, could achieve extraordinary quality and productivity. In this one visit, Adam Smith got to the heart of successful capitalism and management practice: specialisation and the subdivision of labour.

From Adam Smith to Henry Ford it was a very small intellectual leap. Ford swept away the artisan car builders by installing and perfecting the production line. As with the pin makers of Gloucester, he discovered that low-skilled but well-organised workers could achieve quality and quantity beyond the reach of any artisan.

The power of process reengineering was demonstrated by Dell. Michael Dell, as a young graduate, took on the might of IBM, Apple, Toshiba, HP and Compaq in the PC market. He had nothing going for him. Perhaps out of desperation, because he could not afford to have any stock, he decided to sell his computers to order and direct to the public. In one fell swoop he had reengineered the entire industry as follows:

▶ Traditional PC process flow: make, then hope to sell.

▶ Dell PC process flow: sell, then hope to make.

This is reengineering made simple, beyond the wire diagrams of process reengineers. The effect of this one change was to:

▶ eliminate all finished stock

▶ make growth cash positive: customers pay you before you pay your suppliers

- eliminate losses from unsold stock, write-downs and fire sales
- eliminate the need for sophisticated sales forecasting tools
- reduce costs by eliminating expensive resellers
- gain very good and fast knowledge about customer and market trends
- beat the competition.

Good reengineering has two characteristics which Dell showed:

1   It is simple, not complicated.

2   It is focused on the market pressures not internal pressures.

Most process redesign fails these two tests.

4 Changing how people are measured, rewarded and recognised

Two of the oldest adages in management are still two of the truest: 'You can only control what you measure' and 'You only get what you reward'. Core to the manager's task is to measure and reward the right things. Here are some good ways *not* to do it:

- Measure call centre staff on number of calls handled: allow the customers to suffer from poor service as call centre staff rush to get through each call.

- Minimise warranty claims: watch managers erect huge barriers to customers claiming (must pre-register the product after sale, produce the original till receipt, stamped warranty document and original packaging, pay for the postage to Vladivostock, produce evidence that the fault is not subject to any of the 317 exemption clauses in the warranty document and then have the submission signed and approved by all eight of your great grandparents).

- Measure bank calling officers on the volume of loans advanced: then discover that lending money is easy, but getting it back is difficult if you have not paid proper attention to loan quality.

- Measure software writers on KLOCs (thousands of lines of code written): get huge amounts of complicated code which is hard to change instead of fewer, more elegant and more robust code. Measure book writers the same way and you would be in trouble.

The only simple answer to the question 'How should I measure performance' is 'Measure it well.' This is as simple as it is unhelpful. Sometimes, questions are more helpful than answers. Here are the key questions to ask:

▶ What is important to the organisation as a whole currently? This creates the context for setting and refocusing reward and measures in your area. Make sure your goals align with the corporate drive for customer retention, or cost reduction, or rapid growth of skills, staff and sales.

▶ What do I really need to measure? Be careful what you wish for. Remember King Midas in Greek mythology wished that all he touched would turn to gold. He cursed his wish when he found his food, wine, wife and mistresses turning to gold. In reality, you will need a mixture of financial, market, organisation and development measure (see the box below).

▶ How will people react? Think through the consequences of human behaviour (see above). People will take the shortest route to your goal, and short cuts are not always good.

▶ How will I recognise and reward performance? Human nature is curious here. People tend to spend disproportionate emotional energy on what is visible and discretionary. This means that core salary does not drive performance. But bonuses, prizes, company cars, titles and perks receive huge amounts of attention. These are important because they are visible to colleagues and they feel like something we can control directly.

Putting in place effective measurement systems: from data to information

It was the trip on the elevator to the CEO that got me worried about the company measurement systems. At the third floor a porter pushed a low loader into the elevator with about 30kg of computer printout. I asked him what it was. 'This week's reports for Steve (the CEO),' he said cheerfully. Steve did not even like reading.

We both went to see Steve, who groaned at the gigabytes of garbage which had just come through the door.

So we sat down and I asked him to draw up on one side of paper the measures he really wanted to see each week. The important stuff fitted easily onto one sheet of paper. We then started to trawl through the computer printout and found that what he really wanted was not in all the data he received. Inadvertently, we had discovered the balanced scorecard, but lacked the wit to copyright it. The information Steve required answered four basic questions:

1 How are we doing financially? (lagging indicator of performance)

2 How are we doing in the marketplace? (current indicator of performance)

3 How are we doing internally: staff, operations, quality? (current indicator of performance)

4 What's new: tests, pilots, research, key projects? (future indicator of performance)

At this point we started a revolution. We cascaded Steve's sheet of paper down the organisation: each manager would amend it to focus on the detail of their area while ensuring they gathered data which was needed at the top. To start with, many of the sheets of paper were frighteningly blank: no one knew what was happening. Over the following months the relevant information began to flow and management started to regain proper control over the business.

5 Changing how people behave

Cultural revolutions normally fail badly. Think of Mao Tse-tung and 50 million dead. There are good reasons why cultural revolutions fail:

▶ Culture change is normally an attack on the majority: culture represents the informal rules of success and survival in your organisation. Attacking the majority is not a good start. Attacking what is perceived to be at least a survivable model of behaviour does not make it any better.

▶ Culture change is about how people behave. Changing behaviour is an attack on people's personal behaviour. Personal attacks are not the best way to enthuse people.

▶ Cultural change programmes often confuse the ends and the means. The purpose of most organisations is not to produce happy employees. Happy and productive employees are a means to achieve some other end for the organisation.

▶ The process of cultural change is often mismanaged. It may not involve 50 million dead, but it can involve lots of touchy-feely, introspective and interpersonal events which are highly divisive. Some people love the events and claim their lives have been transformed. Other people find the event makes their skin crawl.

Having trashed most cultural programmes, it is now time to praise them. In context and done well they can be essential. There are many organisations where the culture has become deeply dysfunctional. These are the organisations that turn on its head the old adage that 'organisations help ordinary people achieve extraordinary things'. There are far too many organisations which help extraordinary people achieve ordinary things.

It is mainly legacy organisations which are at risk of cultural dysfunction. They grow fat and happy. They get caught in old ways. For a while, this does not matter. They are so strong and dominant in the market that they appear invincible. Then an upstart comes along and changes the rules of the game. The first reaction from the giant is denial. Denial continues until panic or expiration. Panic at least gives a chance of survival.

If you are tempted to start or get involved in a cultural change programme, then there are a few guides to success:

▶ Attack culture crabwise: from the side on. Focus the overt efforts on the business goal, which most people can rally behind. To achieve that goal you will need to put in place a number of enabling activities, which will include rewards, measures, how we work, skills and more. Behaviours are embedded in this.

▶ Be relentlessly positive. Celebrate all the right behaviours. If a shop assistant gives a disgruntled shopper a refund, celebrate the assistant's initiative and customer focus (if that is what you want to achieve). Do not attack everyone else for lack of initiative or customer focus. Slowly, people will get the message about what is valued in the organisation.

▶ Use cultural change levers. Reward and measurement systems are very powerful at driving behaviour. If the rewards are 100 per cent commission, do not be surprised if you have a high-performing and low-ethics sales force.

▶ Lead from the front. People will listen politely to speeches about culture, because they have to. Round the coffee machine they will quickly decide whether the speech was rhetoric or reality. To make it real, you have to support your words with decisions, especially tough decisions.

Values into action

The new headteacher wanted to instil a sense of respect for the individual. The leadership team talked this through and liked the idea, but no one really knew what it meant. Then one day a classroom teacher gave a whole class detention because one individual stole something, and no one owned up. The head teacher asked how a whole class detention showed respect for the individual. There were no more whole class detentions after that.

Meanwhile, the PE teacher had a real reputation for pushing the pupils. She seemed to believe in ritual humiliation of the fat and the asthmatic. That was not respect for the individual either. The PE teacher would not budge on her standards. She soon decided to leave, and they brought in another PE teacher who helped all the pupils, not just the fittest.

Slowly, the culture of the school changed. There was no one great break-through event, no need for the transformative conference dealing with personal and interpersonal behaviour. Instead, all the staff learned together what they really meant by respect for the individual. Because they felt they owned the journey, rather than it being dictated to them, they backed it and it worked.

CHAPTER

5

MQ skills:

managing your journey

Management is an art: it always has been, always will be. There will never be a scientific formula which unlocks the secrets of management in quite the way that $e = mc^2$ unlocked physics. If there was a single formula, we would all have it and we would land up in a competitive stalemate. Everyone would be applying the same formula. Fortunately, people are different, situations are different, actions are different and the world is always changing. There are a million ways to succeed, and as many ways to fail. This makes management the challenge it is. The consequence is that each manager has to learn his or her own rules of survival and success. Any book or course can only give a manager a few more ideas, some different perspectives and a few tools and techniques to try.

Each person will build his or her own, unique, version of MQ: management quotient. It will be as unique as DNA or finger prints. This means that managers need to acquire three essential MQ skills:

▶ Acquiring MQ: how to learn success
▶ Employing MQ: uses and abuses
▶ Decoding the success formula: happy endings.

5.1 Acquiring MQ: how to learn success

Managers are given very little help in becoming managers. Schools teach nothing about political skills and precious little about emotional skills. Arguably, they teach precisely the wrong intellectual skills: they ask students to work alone and produce rational answers to predetermined questions where there is a clear answer. Any manager who expects to work alone producing rational answers to predetermined questions is either going to have a very short managerial career or is going to become an actuary.

Schools, and business schools, are in the business of teaching explicit knowledge. The problem is that they never teach us how to think. They can teach maths, English, physics and double-entry book-keeping. But thinking simply does not exist as a discipline. It is assumed that if we can do algebra and write a grammatical sentence, then we can think effectively. The evidence of daily life shows that this is a mistake. Alienated youths on the street who resolve disputes by relying on a knife are in the same category as the defensive manager who resolves disputes by relying on authority: neither of them has the mental training to know how to resolve such everyday differences effectively.

The problem continues within organisations. Our research asked managers to pick their two most valuable sources of learning about management from the following list:

- books
- courses
- peers
- bosses
- role models
- experience.

Some 99 per cent of respondents failed to mention books or courses: the only person who really valued books was the only one who had not graduated from high school. In that one finding, the entire leadership and management development industry is in danger of disappearing in a puff of irrelevance. For an author of a book on management, it is seriously bad news. The challenge is to make any book relevant, readable and practical.

Before discovering how to help people develop their MQ, it is worth looking at how and why current efforts fail. Many organisations do good professional development around technical skills: helping people learn the trade or craft of their industry be it law, accounting, bond trading, engineering or accounting. But when it comes to learning IQ, EQ and PQ participants suddenly discover they are needed elsewhere that day. The CIPD (Chartered Institute of Personnel and Development) found that the most common excuses were:

- they are too busy at work
- family or personal commitments
- they are insufficiently motivated

▶ resistance from line managers

▶ insufficient culture of learning at work.

These excuses need a little translation, which is provided below:

▶ they are too busy at work (= not a priority)

▶ family or personal commitments (= not a priority)

▶ they are insufficiently motivated (= not a priority)

▶ resistance from line managers (= not a priority for the boss)

▶ insufficient culture of learning at work (= not a priority for anyone).

Lack of time never means lack of time: it means lack of priority. If the same individuals were offered a hot date with their favourite movie or sports star and a million dollars, the chances are that they could shuffle their very busy schedules to make the date.

Management training does not quite have the same allure as a hot date and a million dollars for at least two reasons:

1 Most management training is not very good from the participant's perspective.

2 Training assumes that the participant is deficient in whatever they are learning: this is a sign of weakness that few people care to admit to.

Our research shows that most managers learn from peers, bosses, role models and experience. This makes sense to most people. We see someone mess up and quietly make a note not to step on that particular landmine. We see someone else do something really well and this time we make a note to try and repeat the trick ourselves. Piece by piece we beg, borrow and steal little bits of management DNA from the people and events we encounter. The result is that we build up our own unique management DNA which programmes how we behave under most management situations.

The process of acquiring DNA is highly effective. We do not learn the theory of what should work in general. We learn what works in practice in our particular trade. The investment banker learns to love risk. To civil servants, risk is like kryptonite: they will do everything to manage away risk. The banker and the civil servant are learning opposite lessons and they are both learning the right thing. The practice of what works always trumps the theory of what should work. Practice beats theory every time.

But there is a dark side to this random walk of building your own personalised management DNA. The three major problems are:

1   the wrong experiences

2   the wrong role models

3   the wrong context.

If managers learn from role models and experience, it is essential that they get the right role models and experience. If they get poor role models and poor experiences, they get poor learning. In every organisation there are a few bosses whose dark reputation precedes them: you may have to work for them but few people want to work for them. There are also the nightmare assignments from which few people are expected to escape unscathed.

The random walk of learning from experience can lead to management heaven or management hell, depending on what people and events managers bump into on their journey. There has to be a better way of developing MQ: management quotient.

This book helps the management journey by structuring and accelerating it. Instead of hoping to learn from random experiences, the book gives managers the frameworks which they need to make sense of what they are seeing, experiencing and learning. For weak managers, frameworks are prisons: they mindlessly apply the same formula regardless of the circumstances. They are process prisoners and the frameworks are the prison walls. For strong managers, frameworks let them climb the experience curve faster: the framework becomes an aid to thinking, not a substitute for thinking.

5.2 Employing MQ: uses and abuses

MQ is a simple framework to help you understand the management potential of yourself and your colleagues. It breaks management down into a set of skills which everyone can learn. These are the skills which managers need to make things happen through other people. By way of summary, here is a simple assessment tool to try on yourself and your colleagues. The assessment tool tracks the skills outlined in each chapter, so you can refer back to the relevant sections where necessary. How many of the skills can you honestly say you possess at present?

Skill tracking assessment tool

IQ skills: dealing with tasks, problems and money

2.1 *Starting at the end*: sees the desired outcome for self and for others, simplifies issues by focusing on the end and drives towards it.

2.2 *Achieving results*: sets clear expectations of what can be achieved by when and then delivers them: takes responsibility and has a clear claim to fame.

2.3 *Making decisions*: quickly learns what works and what fails in the business (acquires business sense and intuition) and has a bias towards action.

2.4 *Solving problems*: focus on workable solutions, not perfect solutions; solves problems with and through other people, building their buy-in and support in the process.

2.5 *Strategic thinking*: understands the priorities of senior management and aligns personal agenda in support of the broader business agenda.

2.6 *Setting budgets*: sets realistic expectations upwards, stretching expectations downwards; manages the politics of the budget cycle well.

2.7 *Managing budgets*: sets expectations early to avoid unpleasant surprises; phases spending to ensure essential investment is made early in the year.

2.8 *Managing costs*: is ready for the year-end squeeze; knows where the fat lies; negotiates effectively over any budget revisions.

2.9 *Surviving spreadsheets*: understands the key numbers for the business and consistently tests and challenges assumptions by using them.

2.10 *Knowing numbers*: understands how to use numbers to persuade; uses validation process to build buy-in and support for a case.

EQ skills: dealing with people

3.1 *Motivating people*: demonstrates a real interest in the team and has willing followers.

3.2 *Influencing people*: is able to listen well, understand other people's agendas and builds coalitions in support of action by aligning different agendas across the organisation.

3.3 *Coaching*: helps others discover what works for them; recognises that different people succeed in different ways; does not force own style onto others.

3.4 *Delegating*: delegates meaningful, stretching tasks as well as routine tasks; sets clear and consistent expectations; does not delegate the blame.

3.5 *Handling conflict*: defuses conflict rather than inflames it; recognises which battles are worth fighting and avoids the unnecessary ones.

3.6 *Giving informal feedback*: develops team members by giving prompt and positive feedback; moves from problems to solutions and action.

3.7 *Managing yourself*: is aware of what motivates self, is aware of how he or she impacts on others and adjusts to different situations and people well.

3.8 *Using time effectively*: has clear goals and priorities in the short, medium and long term and is not deflected unnecessarily from them: focuses on achievement, not activity.

3.9 *Surviving the management marathon*: retains control of events, even in adversity; rests and relaxes enough and constantly reflects, learns and grows.

3.10 *Learning the right behaviour*: role models the behaviours most valued in the organisation; is consistently positive, professional and people focused.

PQ skills: making things happen

4.1 *The seven key power sources*: understands how to be of value to the organisation and acquires the relevant capabilities and power to be of value.

4.2 *Acquiring power*: has a claim to fame, and stakes the claim; actively seeks out and asks for or takes the appropriate opportunities; does not wait to be asked.

4.3 *Building power networks*: knows where power lies; builds alliances with the key power brokers; seeks positions which will enhance long-term career prospects.

4.4 *Using power*: seeks power not for status, but for the opportunity to achieve more on a bigger stage; focus on contributions, not rewards.

4.5 *The art of unreasonable management*: knows when and how to fight battles and to stretch people beyond their comfort zones.

4.6 *Saying 'no' to your boss*: finds positive alternatives and uses smart questions to get the boss to change direction without having to say 'no' directly.

4.7 *Power and integrity:* commands widespread trust based on honesty, even in awkward situations, and on consistent delivery of promises.

4.8 *Taking control*: has a clear and compelling vision of what is important, what must change and how it will change.

4.9 *Managing change*: clear focus on building and maintaining a political coalition in support of change; focus on benefits, business case, actions and outcomes not on problems; people-focused more than project-focused.

4.10 *People and change*: manages individuals through the pain and emotion of change well.

Many of these skills will not exist in a formal assessment system, which is why formal assessment systems are so often a source of frustration. They help no one understand what is really important in an effective manager. Although management is everywhere, few people have dared to define it and even fewer teach it: you can learn accounting, finance and marketing and still not know how to manage. This book, and the assessment tool above, helps you cut through the noise and understand the critical skills and interventions every manager needs if they are to succeed in practice.

5.3 Decoding the success formula: happy endings

In 1989 Freddie Mercury and Queen released 'The Miracle' and sang, 'I want it all and I want it now.' Nowadays we want more, and we want it faster. This is great news for the modern-day medicine men selling their cure-alls in a bottle. Except that nowadays we are more sophisticated and call the cure things like 'alternative medicines', 'holisitic treatments' or, for businesses, 'reengineering', 'core competencies', 'value innovation' and 'co-creation'. We learn the word, take the medicine and. . . nothing happens.

People and businesses have been taking quack cures not for decades, but for millennia. We have moved on from sacrificing sheep to the gods, but we still want The Miracle.

The good news for managers is that there is no miracle five-day course that will turn a disillusioned worker into a brilliant manager. You cannot succeed on just five minutes a day, even if there is a promise of your money back. The lack of an instant, universal formula for managerial success is good news for at least three reasons:

1   If there was an instant formula, everyone would have it: you would have no competitive advantage against other managers and you would be left looking for another instant formula to shine relative to other managers.

2   If there was a single formula, management would be a very dull matter of mindlessly applying the same formula day in and day out. There are days when a simple formula would be preferable to the exciting crises of management, but few people would want to do the same thing the same way for 40 or more years.

3   If there was a single formula, we would all have to conform to it like brainwashed zombies. Some managers already behave like brain-washed zombies. The rest of us value being who we are, playing to our strengths and carefully bypassing our (very few and minor) weak-nesses.

So we have to make up our own formula for success. We look, listen and learn from our experience and from others'. We copy, steal and adapt little bits of management DNA from everyone else. We copy what we like and hope to avoid messing up the way others mess up: we can all find enough creative ways to mess ourselves up without copying other people's faults as well. Eventually, we build up our own unique management DNA which works in our own unique environment. The perfect manager is as unlikely as the perfect predator: we are as dependent on finding the right context as the polar bear and the lion are on finding their right contexts.

As we go on our separate management journeys, we need something to help us on our way. This book, any book, cannot pretend to give the universal solution to all management challenges. But used wisely, it can help you accelerate your learning from experience and hence your journey to success.

How to Manage does not give a universal formula for success. It does much better than that. It helps you decode your unique success formula.

Wherever you go, enjoy your journey.

Index

achieving results: performance and
perceptions 16, 22, 227
fix the baseline 22, 23
manage for results 22, 25
play the numbers game 22, 23–4
work harder 22
work smarter 22, 23
acquiring MQ: how to learn success
223–6
acquiring power: shining a light on the
dark arts,
playing for power
ask for it 167, 170–2, 228
take it 172
power of the pen 172–3
Nike strategy: just do it 172,
173–5
work for it 167
build a claim to fame 167–8
focus on the moments of truth
168–70
power and the heart of the empire
161–3
power network: career management
165–7
where to find power 161
power at the outposts of empire 161,
163–5
believe nothing 163–4
manage perceptions 164
stay in touch 164
art of unreasonable management:
ruthlessness 187–8, 229
how to be unreasonable and ruthless
189

assignments and promotions 188,
190–1
budget negotiations 188, 189
how to deal with the ruthless boss
191–3
target setting 188, 190
team formation 188, 190
when to be unreasonable and
ruthless 188
automatic voice response (AVR)
38, 40

betterfastercheaper 23, 61, 194, 213
Boston Consulting Group, matrix
mania 52
BP, high-potential graduates work in
CEO's office 162
brainstorming 45
Branson, Richard 15–16
Buddhist monks 139–40
building power networks: becoming
irreplaceable 175, 202, 229
roles within your network 176–7
coaches 176, 181
gatekeepers 176, 178–9
the godfather 176, 177–8, 200
the player 176, 177
soldiers 176, 179
technocrats 176, 179–81
users 176, 178

call centres, rational management in
21st century 6
Canon 51, 53
capitalism, betterfastercheaper 23, 61

CEOs 16, 23, 33, 104, 199, 216
  budget 56, 73, 158
  Maslow's hierarchy of needs 81
  measurement systems 216–17
  power 156, 175
  teamwork 49
  valley of death experience 202
  working in office of 162
change, attitudes to 199–200
change management 206
Chartered Institute of personnel and
    Development (CIPD) 224
Chicago rules 47
Cirque du Soleil 53
Clausedwitz, on diplomacy 104
coaching 30, 84, 101, 112, 141, 169,
    211
  coaching: no more training 96–7,
    228
    objectives 97
    options 97, 98
    outcomes 97, 98–9
    overview 97–8
COBOL, fate of 159
Collins, Colonel Tim 104
cost-benefit analysis,
  payback period 37
  return on investment (ROI) 37–8
cultural change 217–19

Darwin, Charles: activity versus
    achievement 124
decoding the success formula: happy
    endings 229–31
delegating: doing better by doing less
    99, 228
  discuss the process 100–1, 200
  follow up 101–2
  know your team 100, 200

  set clear objectives 100
  work out what you can delegate 99
Dell 50, 214–15
Deming, W. Edwards 7–8
dysfunctional conflict 102–3
Dyson, design is where power lies
    162

earnings per share (EPS) 61
EasyJet 50
employing MQ: uses and abuses
    226–7
EQ (motional management) 7–9,155,
    207, 224
EQ skills: dealing with people 77–8,
    108, 228
Europe, safety recall 61

fast-food restaurants, rational
    management in 21st century
    6
fear, uncertainty and doubt (FUD)
    200
FedEx 50
financial data, importance of 59
financial quotient (FQ) 17
financial skills,
  budget utility and futility 60
  managing budgets 54
  managing costs 54
  playing the numbers game 54
  setting budgets 54
  surviving spreadsheets 54
Ford, Henry, car making 6, 214

Gates, Bill 15–16, 189
GE, 'lemonade stands' 163
giving informal feedback: making the
    negative positive 109, 228

principle one: give positive feedback 109–10

principle two: make constructive feedback constructive 110

  be specific, not general and focus on behaviour not the person 110, 111

  find the right time and the right place 110–11

  pause 110, 111–12

  solve the problem and move to the next steps 110, 112–13

GMAT (common sense test) 4

GM and Ford, finance is where the power is 158, 162

Goleman, Daniel, *Emotional Intelligence: Why it can matter more than IQ* 7

graduates, seek high-stress employers 132–3

Green, Philip 29–30

handling conflict: from fear to ear 102–3, 202, 228

  let the storm blow itself out 106

    agree the problem 94, 106, 107–8

    empathise 106, 107

    resolve the way forward 106, 108–9

  principle one: know which battles to fight 103–4

  principle two: from fear to ear 104–5

    buy time to think 105

    regain personal control 105

Hawthorn experiments 142

Honda 53

How to Manage 5, 10–11, 231

HR 8, 34, 58, 68, 73, 102, 160, 164, 171, 206

IBM 163, 214

Industrial Revolution, evolution of management 5

influencing,

  the listening rule 95

  the partnership rule 95

influencing people: how to sell anything 84–5, 228

  principles of influencing people 85

    fear 85–6, 89, 176

    greed 85–6, 89, 176

    idleness 85, 87, 89, 176

    risk 85, 87–9, 177

  process of influencing people 89

    agree the problem: what is the fear we are dealing with? 90–1, 93–4

    close 92, 93–4

    explain how it works: make it easy for them 92, 93–4

    outline the benefits of resolving the problem 91–2, 93–4

    pre-empt any objections: remove the risk 92

    preparation and the social introduction 89–90, 93

    summary of the process 93

integrity, at the heart of performance culture 195

internal rate of return (IRR) 39

interpersonal skills 4

involuntary redundancies 64

IQ (intelligence quotient) 4–5, 8–10, 37, 155, 224

  financial theory and 18

  project management 206–7

rational management 5–6

    solve problem and agree way forward
        108

IQ skills: dealing with problems, tasks
        and money 15–17, 227

IT consultants, fear and 86

Japan 7, 31, 61–2, 164–5, 214

Jobs, Steve 15

'Just a Minute' 213

kaizen (continuous improvement) 7,
        64–5, 214

Kim, Chan 53

knowing the numbers: playing the
        numbers game 69, 227

    assumptions game 69–70

    averages game 69, 70–1

    baseline game 69, 71

        declining baseline 71–2

        false baseline 73

    validation game 69, 73–4

learning the right behaviours: what
        managers really want 142–5,
        228

    people focus 145

    positive outlook 145–7

        action 147, 148–9

        analysis 147, 148

        answers 147, 148

        apathy 147, 148

    professional behaviour 149

        individual 151

        institutional 150–51

lemming syndrome 53

MacGregor, *The Human Side of Enterprise*
    80

Machiavelli, *The Prince* 9, 77

McKinsey, 'One Firm Firm' 174

making decisions: acquiring intuition
        fast 17, 25, 227

    analysis over action 27

    decision making in practice 28

        does someone know the answer
            anyway? 28, 31–2

        is there a pattern I recognise?
            28–30

        who does this decision matter to
            and why? 28, 30

            important for one of your
                bosses 30

            important to another colleague
                31

            important to a team member
                30

            important to you and your
                agenda 31

    decision making principles 25

        bias for action over analysis 25, 27

        hiding behind other people 27

        prefer practical to perfect solutions
            25

        seeking perfection over practicality
            27

        shedding responsibility 28

        solve the problem with other
            people 25

        take responsibility 26–7

management 3

    21st century slavery 165

    an art 223

    change and 199

    difficulty of defining 229

    DNA 10, 211, 225–6, 230

    has become harder and more
        ambiguous 3

has become more demanding and rewarding 182

hierarchy of needs 82–3

high commitment workplace 7

Industrial Revolution 5

seriously hard work 130

management intelligence, differs from academic intelligence 16

managers 3–4, 15

  attracted to power 162

  averse to risk 26

  career network checklist 166

  characteristics of ideal 142–5

  decisive 25

  effective need to vary their pitch and pace 137

  effective start at the end 18

  elements of working day 15

  finding it difficult to delegate 99

  foundations for 16–17

  good are selectively unreasonable 57, 187

  good 'have hinterland' 211

  gurus and problems of burn-out and stress 130–1

  how to deal with the fear reaction 105

  lesson for newly promoted 96

  major part of challenge is political 17

  most learn from peers, bosses, role models and experience 225

  most value resource is time 182

  need IQ, EQ and PQ 5

  need to negotiate for support 175

  pattern recognition 29

  people skills 210–11

  perfect unlikely 230

  real are three dimensional 8–9

  responsibility and 26

  role to make things happen through other people 24

  skills needed by politically intelligent 155–6

  strategy and 49

  understanding how you affect other people 115

  use of numbers to support their case 55

managing budgets: the annual dance routine,

  know your numbers in advance of official data 58, 227

  manage communications well

    avoid boasting 59

    avoid surprises 59

    don't whine, negotiate 59

  prepare for a rainy day

    48/52 rule 58

    sandbag 58

  prioritise your spending 59

    discretionary spending 59

    essential investments 59

managing change: people, not projects 199–200, 229

  managing the change journey 200–2

  managing resistance 200, 202–3

  offering resistance 200, 203–4

    be positive 205

    buy time 204

    do a deal 205

    do nothing 204

    get help 205–6

managing costs: minimising pain 60–2, 227

  hard squeeze 61, 64

  making real change 62, 64–5

  play the game 61, 62

    KKK 62

play it the right way 62

sandbagging 62

timing 62

two thing you can ask for 63

pretend to make real change 62, 65

scoreboarding 66–7

squeeze the balloon 65

soft squeeze 61, 63

managing yourself: personal EQ 113, 228

self-adjustment 117

be adaptable 118

control your own emotions 117

learn and grow 118

explicit knowledge and learning 119

tacit knowledge or know-how 119

self-awareness 114, 115–17

self motivation 114–15

Maslow, hierarchy of needs 80–3, 85–6

MBA tools, managers and 15–16

Microsoft, why highly profitable 52

motivating people: creating willing followers,

basic theories 79–80, 228

motivation practice: the magic rule 83–4

the sophisticated theories 80–3

MQ: managing your journey 223

MQ: the management quotient 9–11

negotiation skills 55–7, 63, 175, 188

nemawashi, consensus-based decision making in Japan 31

Nokia 48

Orwell, George 125–6

pattern recognition, buying decisions 28–30

peer group learning 211

people and change: through the valley of death 206–7, 229

changing how people are measured, rewarded and recognised 207, 215–17

changing how people behave 207, 217–19

changing how people do things: skills 207, 209–12

changing how people and tasks are organised 207, 212–15

changing what people do 207–9

emotional aspects 208

political aspects 208

rational aspects of reorganising 208

perfect solution, does not exist 25

performance, understanding causes of good or poor important 34

Personnel Today, findings on internet use 121

political skills, about the organisation and action 155

politics, in organisations 9

Porter, Michael, Five Forces analysis 52

Postscript: your chance to lead 233

power and integrity: from morality to survival 195–6, 229

PQ: (political quotient) 4–5, 8–9, 18, 37, 108, 207, 224

PQ skills: making things happen 155–6, 228–9

Prahalad and Hamel 51, 53, 163

Premier Brands, orphan brands and 53

problems,
  cost are always symptom of
    something else 34
  solve with other people 25–6
process change 212–13
Procter & Gamble 28–30, 89, 162, 205
professional service firms, power lies
    with the clients 162
project managers, change managers 206

question, 'why?' to unearth root of
    problem 34

Ramaswamy, Venkat 53
reengineering 213–15, 230
reorganisation, IQ, EQ and PQ 8, 207
responsibility 26–8
risk 26–7, 87–8, 199, 206
ROI (return on investment) 37–9
role models 225–6

saying 'no' to your boss: surviving
    insanity 193, 229
  people 194–5
  priorities 194
  process 194
scientific management 5–6
setting budgets: politics of performance
    55, 227
  adjustments 56–7
  anchoring the budget discussion
    55–6
seven key power sources: building a
    power base 156–7, 228
  access 157, 160
  customers 157, 159
  information 157, 158–9
  money 157, 158
  permissions 157, 160

scarce resources 157, 161
skills 157, 159
Shakespeare, *Julius Caesar* as politics
    dramatised 9
Sinclair, Clive, the C5 vehicle 88
Smith, Adam, *Wealth of Nations* 21,
    214
solving problems: prisons and
    frameworks 386
  focus on causes not symptoms 32,
    33–4, 227
  know your problem 32–3
  prioritise the problems 35
  problem-solving tools 35–6
    cost-benefit analysis 35, 36–7
      NPV (net present value) 37,
        39–40
      payback period 37
      ROI (return on investment)
        37–9
      sensitivity analysis 40
    creative problem solving 36, 45–7
    field force analysis 36, 42
    fishbone/mind maps 36, 44–5
    multifactor/trade-off/grid analysis
      36, 42–4
    SWOT analysis 35, 36, 41
South West Airlines 50
stakeholders 21
starting at the end: focusing on
    outcomes 16, 18–19, 227
  what are the consequences of this
    course of action? 18, 21
  what are the minimum number of
    steps required to get there?
    18, 20–1
  what outcomes does the other
    person expect from this
    situation? 18, 20

what outcomes do I want to achieve
from this situation ? 18, 19
strategic thinking; floors, romantics
and the classics 47–8, 227
know how to think strategically 50
play the strategy game 50–2
understanding nature of strategy 52
classical 52–3
postmodern 53
understand strategic relevance of
your own activities 48–9
stress,
checklist of excessive 134
overload and break-down zone 132
Sun-Tsu, *The Art of War* 103–4, 188
surviving the management marathon:
from days to decades 130,
228
reflect 135, 141–2
regain control 135–6
relax 135, 137–8
controlled breathing 138, 139–41
positive visualisation 138, 139
progressive physical relaxation
138–9
rest 135, 136–7
stress and the challenge of the
management marathon 131–5
surviving spreadsheets: assumption not
maths 67–9, 227

taking control: telling stories 196–7,
229
this is how we are going to get there
196, 198
this is how you can help 196, 198–9
this is where we are going 196–8
Taylor, Frederick, *Principles of Scientific
Management, The* 6–7

technology 120–1, 182
Thai tapioca test 171–2
thinking 223, 226
Thorndike, E.L., 'social intelligence' 7
time, lack of means lack of priority 225
time management and the cookie jar
127–8
Toyota and Nissan, engineering is
where the power lies 162
TQM (total quality management) 214

unintended consequences of results
obsession 23–4
USA, litigation 61
using power: setting your agenda
181–2, 229
personal tests of the right agenda
182–3
professional tests of the right agenda
183–4
how important is this agenda to
the organisation 184
how likely are we to succeed? 185
the wrong godfather 185, 186
the wrong problem 185
the wrong process 185, 187
the wrong team 185, 186–7
using time effectively: activity versus
achievement 119–20, 228
dealing with the urgent stuff 129–30
do it now: avoid procrastination 123,
130
do it right first time every time 122,
129
handle each communication once
122–3, 129–30
time effectiveness 124
focusing on the important stuff
126–9

knowing what you want to achieve
125–6
time efficiency 120–1

Wall Street saying 103

workers 3, 6–7, 79–80
work-life balance 22, 131
WPP (advertising conglomerate) 48

Xerox 51